MYSELF HELP

MYSELF HELP

A Psychotherapist's Journey
toward
Authenticity

Dana Anderson

BALBOA.
PRESS

A DIVISION OF HAY HOUSE

ISBN: 978-1-4525-5958-2 (sc)
ISBN: 978-1-4525-5959-9 (e)
ISBN: 978-1-4525-5960-5 (hc)

Library of Congress Control Number: 2012917774

Balboa Press books may be ordered through booksellers or by contacting:

Balboa Press
A Division of Hay House
1663 Liberty Drive
Bloomington, IN 47403
www.balboapress.com
1-(877) 407-4847

Printed in the United States of America

Balboa Press rev. date: 10/17/2012

Acknowledgments

Throughout this process, their were many who helped me along the way. My dearest friends, Sally Archambault, Lesley Claire, Diana Damon, Carlee Ferrari, and Linda Dew-Heirsoux, all of whom offered their time, advice, and continued support. And another friend, Leilani Schweitzer who crossed my path and the light of synchronicity shone. I don't believe this book would've happened without knowing this woman.

I'd like to thank my cover designer, Milan Sperka of MeshCreative in Reno, Nevada was very helpful and expedient partner. I look forward to our future projects. And previously mentioned, Sally Archambault, whose computer and design talents she made readily available to me. A real gift.

Most importantly, I am grateful for my many clients in Napa, California and the surrounding Bay Area; and in the Reno/Tahoe area, including parts farther away. These brave persons inspired me and provided the stories that illuminated my own process.

And lastly, my family, who had to make compromises and was continuously supportive during this process—particularly my husband. I am grateful for their patience, work, concessions—there were simply times when I was unavailable—and mostly, their love. I am blessed.

Dedication

In memory of my brother, Douglas Carl Anderson, and my best friend, Scott Edward Kaelin. May I feel their light again and again. And my husband, Rich, who was sent from above.

Contents

PART 1

OH, GOOD GRIEF

My Not-So-Pretty Prologue

This is a book on grief, authenticity, and spirituality. It is opinion and intuition, not research and fact. Following my most recent relocation across state lines, I was increasingly aware of what I would have called my own hypocrisy. At least it felt like hypocrisy, which I eventually understood to be my personal "authenticity work."

I've done well as a psychotherapist. I know how to help my clients. I know how to help my family. I can help myself, but I don't always do it. In fact, I sometimes consciously and rebelliously do the opposite. And then I sit with my clients and listen. And think. And listen and think. And often I provide insight. I may even tell them what to do. And it works. I have had great successes in my practice, and I am proud of them. Yet sometimes, I don't follow my own advice. I don't always do (or not do) what I think I should or shouldn't do.

It hasn't always been that way. There was a time when I was walking the walk. But then came a *complication*.

This book is an admission, a witness, a sharing of my virtues and vices. You see, I both believe in and have witnessed transformation—major transformation. I have transformed my "self" in many ways, and yet I discovered a new block—something that kept me from my full potential. I thought I knew what it was—I'm a therapist, for goodness sake. And I have a personal spiritual practice. Then why didn't I just "fix it"? What was stopping me? Something in the past? Perhaps.

When I was in college, studying to be an actress, I went to a psychotherapist and told her my sad childhood story. I told it well, explaining that I wanted to be a great actress and that I was aware I had "issues." I wanted to work through these issues so that I could be a fabulous and *authentic* artist. The psychotherapist was so impressed that she sent me on my merry way after only one session. I was healed.

Of course, I wasn't really healed. Later, I learned that what I had done was to intellectualize all my problems—very well. I spoke with such honesty and articulation that I fooled the therapist. The problem was that during that session, I barely felt a thing. I totally avoided what therapists call *affect*. I needed to connect *affect* with my story. I needed to feel something. But I didn't.

This avoidance of feelings went on for some time. Years later, I went into therapy to do my "deep work," so that I could become a fabulous and authentic psychotherapist. I also wanted to figure out how I ended up where I was at the time—divorced. And it worked. I processed my adult-child-of-alcoholic (ACoA) issues (my tendency for codependency), and I became a successful psychotherapist. (Doing personal therapy work is not only mandated by our legal and ethical guidelines, but it also is critical so that a future psychotherapist understands what it's like to be "in the hot seat." Great harm could result from a therapist's not having worked through his or her own personal issues.)

Following my relocation, although I still could help my clients, I began to sense old feelings of guilt (and its ugly sidekick, shame), post-traumatic stress (anxiety), and grief. I returned to behaviors that helped me avoid those feelings. I would have said that "affect" hardly seemed to be an issue, because I'd always been a weeper—an openly emotional person, the classic "bleeding heart." I was a member of Greenpeace at age fourteen and gave money to the American Society for the Prevention of Cruelty to Animals, the World Wildlife Fund, and the Nature Conservancy before I was even old enough to have a bank account. I felt something for everyone and everything. And yet now, I was beginning to wonder, *What was I feeling for myself?*

As an adult child of an alcoholic, I was hyper-vigilant in monitoring my behaviors, making sure I did only a little of something but rarely too much. "Moderation is the key to a good life" was my motto, and moderation applied to both good and bad. I could see myself as the backup singer but not the star. I drank wine but rarely liquor. When I started to shine at something, I backed away. This enabled me to keep feelings like anxiety or guilt at bay and put me in control. I had it all figured out ... or so I thought.

In 2006, I relocated to Reno, Nevada, leaving behind a busy, wait-list practice with a solid reputation in Napa, California. That reputation was based solely on my work with adolescents, though I also specialized in other areas, including trauma and eating disorders. But in this new place, I had no reputation. I needed to rebuild what I'd lost by moving, and I did not anticipate my own grief at the loss of my successful practice. I had no idea how heavily my ego was tied to my reputation. I thought I was above this, having an ego. Of course I wasn't, and I went through a depression during the first year in the new town—a depression I denied. On the outside, I was having fun, fun, fun. Deep down, I was feeling lost, lost, lost, even though I'd convinced myself that I needed a break and moving would be a good thing. (I would write a book!)

I had no idea how deeply ingrained my reputation was in my self-worth. After all, I believed that the greatest benefit of change was opportunity, and I am a seizer (perhaps a Caesar) in this arena. I truly saw this opening as an opportunity to reinvent myself. I'd loved working with teens, but I thought my best work was with women in the area of codependence. My ability to utilize my love of metaphysics only enhanced the potential, and I set out to attract women who were on a higher path of transformation. My "Oprah crowd," I called them.

I ended up attracting women on a path of grief (definitely "Oprah gals"). I began seeing what I had generally referred to as my "trauma" lens as a "grief" lens. It took a move across state lines (of which there'd been many) for me to realize I had grief issues. The residue of grief that caused me to move around more than the average person hadn't been loud enough to shout out, "Hey! You're running from something!" I thought I *had* grieved (or mourned). After all, I'd run the gamut of emotions associated with grief. Apparently, it hadn't been enough.

My mom died from alcoholism when I was eighteen years old. I was in the "invincible" stage common to teenagers, and I went on, I played hard. I became an adrenaline junkie, seeking out situations that would enable me to avoid feelings. I'll explain this in more detail later, but I now believe that I eventually took on a trauma lens as a therapist in order to confine my own emotions in the clinical realm. That enabled me to avoid focusing on my own grief. Eventually, however, I was no longer able to do this. The universe had been telling me in every way possible, "Hey! You're grieving. You should be doing your own grief work." I didn't get it. Until the reinvention. And the *complication*.

The move from California to Nevada made my personal need crystal clear. I could help others, but I still had some of my own demons to work on, and those bastards showed up big time in the new location. I say that, but I tend to exaggerate—it's the ACoA in me. We tend to exaggerate our shame issues, at least with ourselves. Still, my own shame and guilt and grief were preventing me from being my authentic self, and this began to wreak havoc on my psyche.

Fortunately for me, I love to play connect the dots. The spectacles I wear are bifocals: on the top for intentions, and below, synchronicity. This easily creates and reveals what the picture is—even to the blindest of us. And for me, as I believe for everyone, these dots connect us with our true spirit—the divine as it is, both in us and working through us at all times.

Today, I am grateful for this move, for my work, and for my family. I hope to share this story openly and honestly, so that it will help others.

Just a Guy Named Galileo

In the sixteenth century, Galileo Galilei said,

> Philosophy is written in this grand book — I mean the universe — which stands continually open to our gaze, but it cannot be understood unless one first learns to comprehend the language in which it is written. It is written in the language of mathematics, and its characters are triangles, circles, and other geometric figures, without which it is humanly impossible to understand a single word of it; without these, one is wandering about in a dark labyrinth.[1]

For these reasons (so well articulated by Galileo), I include the following supplementary American Psychiatric Association definitions [2](fun stuff!):

Grief: Normal, appropriate emotional response to an external and consciously recognized loss; it is usually time-limited and subsides gradually. To be distinguished from depression. See mourning.

Mourning: Grief: reaction to a loss of a love object (i.e., important person, object, role, status, or anything considered part of one's life) consisting of a process of emotional detachment from that object which frees the subject to find other interests and enjoyments.

Bereavement: Feelings of deprivation, desolation, and grief at the loss of a loved one. The grieving person does not need to seek professional help unless these feelings last for a long period or relief is sought for symptoms such as insomnia.

Depression: When used to describe a mood, depression refers to feelings of sadness, despair, and discouragement. As such, depression may be a normal feeling state. The overt manifestations are highly variable and may be culture specific. Depression may be a symptom seen in a variety of mental or physical disorders, a syndrome of associated symptoms secondary to an underlying disorder, or a specific mental disorder. Slowed thinking, decreased pleasure, decreased purposeful physical depressive syndrome. Depression in children may be indicated by refusal to go to school, anxiety, excessive reaction to separation from parental figures, antisocial behavior, and somatic complaints.

Post-Traumatic Stress Disorder (PTSD): An anxiety disorder in which exposure to an exceptional mental or physical stressor is followed, sometimes immediately and sometimes not until three months or more after the stress, by persistent reexperiencing of the event, avoidance of stimuli associated with the trauma, or numbing of general responsiveness, and manifestations of increased arousal. The trauma typically includes experiencing, witnessing, or confronting an event that involves actual or threatened death or injury, or a threat to the physical integrity of oneself or others, with an immediate reaction of intense fear, helplessness, or horror.

Reexperiencing the trauma may take several forms: recurrent, intrusive, and distressing recollections (images, thoughts, or perceptions) of the event; recurrent distressing dreams of the event; sudden feeling as if the event were recurring or being relived (including dissociative flashback episodes); or intense psychological distress or physiological reactivity if exposed to internal or external cues that symbolize or resemble some part of the event.

The affected person tries to avoid thoughts or feelings associated with the event and anything that might arouse recollection of it. There may be amnesia for an important aspect of the trauma. The person may lose interest in significant activities, feel detached or estranged from others, or have a sense of a foreshortened future.

The person may have difficulty falling or staying asleep, be irritable or have angry outbursts, experience problems concentrating, and have an exaggerated startle response.

My word definitions also come from my *Webster's New Collegiate Dictionary* (hard cover) that is in my office[3] (copyright 1974). I think I picked it up at a yard sale, years ago. This definitely says something about me. I'm a bit of a dinosaur. And I was curious to see how things were defined in 1974. This is one of my neurotic habits—looking up word definitions. Checking my brain (and vocabulary). You see, I come from a *very* articulate family, and sometimes I question whether I actually know the real definitions or just inherited the gift for gab. There are some words I was forced to Google, as my *Webster's* is ... well, how shall we say ... dated. In this case, I chose Wikipedia as my main source, as it is a neat contrast to my antique *Webster's*. I also like that fact that it is indicative of this new world we live in, one I've struggled to join. And I am proud to say, I like it. I'm starting to get comfortable in this century. Okay, it took much more than a decade but who's counting?

Better Start with My Grief Dance

Start (v.): to begin a course or journey

F ive years ago, if someone had referred a grief case to me, I would
have sent him or her to another therapist. A specialist.

"I don't do grief work," I'd have said. "I work with trauma."

Hah. Remarkable. After you read of the loss I've experienced, you might
think I would have gotten this sooner—it astounds me that I didn't see this
grief piece when it was sitting there on the surfaces of all my floors, tables,
and walls. Altars, pictures, collages, art, and tissues. Memories. But I didn't.
Even after my double-whammy grief experience in my midthirties that left
both my brother and my best friend dead (on separate occasions) and left
me limp, I stuck to my trauma lens—it's so wonderful and scientific. Easily
understandable. Trauma, as you will learn, creates a physiological condition.
And this made it even easier to cover up the grief. It took a move to Reno
and a dance with gambling (which I had scarcely done before) for me to get
it. It also took a whole lot of synchronicity.

I had performed varied dances with grief prior to my double-whammy grief experience. First, "ballroom dancing," where I sought romance and intimacy (guys) to buffer and even erase its existence following my mom's death, weeks before my high school graduation. She had battled alcoholism at a time when it was considered a "brown bag" shortfall, a hobo's problem. I don't think the term "disease" was even in effect. I grew up in Michigan, shook hands with Gerald Ford at a wee age when he was one of our state representatives, and was (and still am) deeply moved by Betty Ford's heroism on many issues.

However, Mrs. Ford's tireless and brave work on women's issues came too late for my mom. After her death, it was as if I had on roller skates (Rollerblades came later, and boy, did I love them when they arrived); I was moving a little too fast. I numbly chose a school out of state, where my high school boyfriend and oldest girlfriend were going. After a "trauma" at this small liberal arts college (I was held in my dorm room for several hours—no guns, no rape, just no ability to leave—by a person who had been photographing me from a distance for many months), I transferred to the nearest place I could find. I didn't even apply to University of Michigan, which was quite unusual for my regional upbringing. I defected to Ohio State, where I could get very lost at one of the largest universities on the planet.

Then came "tap dancing," where I attempted to step on and crush all evidence of the existence of grief after a very close college friend died in a tragic house fire; I was twenty-two. We had been together through the death of his father and the wounds of my mother. This was so heartbreaking, as he and his brother died together, days before Christmas. His mom was driving from New Jersey to Ohio at the time of this fire, to be with her boys for Christmas. I can't imagine her grief as she arrived to this heartbreaking scene (no cell phones back then). To this day, twenty-five years later, I think of this mother on Christmas, even though we never met. When I recall receiving the news, I can see how I sunk deeper and deeper into my "play hard" mode. I immediately and unconsciously cut off all ties with college friends (even though one of my best college friends was as deeply wounded as I was) and excused it by a move across country.

Next came "ballet," where I soared to the heavens and gracefully ascended over grief's existence following my beloved grandmother's death. I was deep in denial when my grandmother died. We were close, despite the fact that she was a difficult character. She was also a fantastic lady, a champion for many important causes—and as such, she irritated people. I found myself pausing before mentioning her name, though I was proud of her efforts in conservation. (She taught me many naughty things that involved nail polish and fur coats—you get the picture. She was complicated.)

In the years following her stroke on Nantucket Island, while I was living on the West Coast, I couldn't bring myself to see her "compromised." I carried tremendous guilt about not visiting her for a long time. When I was in my early twenties, my grandmother had asked me to "assist" her to her end, should she need it. In my teens, it seemed undemanding, doable, and natural. As I matured, I evaded the discussions as best I could, but I am sure this contributed to my absence at the end. My grandmother died from starvation; she just stopped eating.

And then there is the long list of bizarre and scary death experiences I had as a child and young adult. I consider this to be my catch-all, freestyle "hip-hop" dancing. This is where I indulged myself and played (partied) in a futile attempt to forget about my grief. I often wonder if my childhood was normal in this way: did everyone come from a middle-class neighborhood where their brother's good friend was electrocuted and died in his shop class in eighth grade? Or did everyone's eight-year-old sister have a friend who was kidnapped and murdered while on a family vacation in Montana? Or an older sister whose good friend was struck by lightning and died on a family vacation? Did everyone live in a county where there was an Oakland County child killer? Was this normal? Again, only a fraction of my whole story.

This leads to the sorrowful and unexpected death of my best, best, best (need I say that a fourth time?) friend, Scott, upon whose own existence I was sorely dependent, and without whom, life surely would not be bearable. He was the one friend I maintained over time and through traumas (my fifteen year friendship). He was the person who knew me inside and out. The one who "got" me. The one who was supposed to be there, *no matter what*. There was no dancing. There was no floor. I had no feet. I had nothing.

Eighteen months later, my brother died. When I first wrote this, I was certain it had been ten months later, and I searched for hard evidence that I was wrong—that's how immediately raw, wounded, and disoriented I was still feeling. I could not hear the music for this dance. Though it was loud, I *would not* hear it. I was angry with my brother. When we were young and frightened—we were eighteen months apart in age—we promised that we would never desert each other. *And we would never become our mother.* We were conscious of this.

I lost Scott to colon cancer when he was thirty-five, around six months after his diagnosis. He had no choice. My brother relapsed and overdosed on crack cocaine. In my mind, he had choice. I had nothing left for him but anger. I chose to sit this one out ... or so I thought.

My high school best friend's mom killed herself, cinching our best-friends status—my own mom was dying slowly from her disease at the time. Yet my best friend from high school and I don't talk today. In fact, we very quickly lost communication right after graduation. There have been a few phone calls over the past thirty years, all of which I remember exactly where I was at the time, but we have no real relationship today. Extraordinarily, I am still in contact (barely, but we each know where the other is) with my high school and on-again/off-again college boyfriend. I know this is about a witnessing. And about history. I don't want to lose this remote connection, because he is the only non–family member I have who knew me when. He is a definite witness.

I could list many more losses that seemed almost normal for me at the time. It had become normal—watching bad things happen. I honestly don't think this is unusual. There also were many moves, including one that was cross-continental, which I'm omitting. (You know, it's even easier to get lost in a foreign country. Actually, as a sixteen-year-old blonde in Paris, 1980, I kind of stood out.) I am now connecting the dots between my losses and my moves—and my address book (or lack thereof). It's an interesting map. I believe all of my moves were related to loss. I define loss broadly in this case as any significant traumatic or grief experience. And unfortunately for me, many people associated with those losses were taken out of my address book.

Merely by being a close friend.

Literally, Labels

Literally (adv.), Literal (adj.): According with the letter of the Scriptures

Label (n.): a slip inscribed and affixed to something for identification or description

I n today's technological world, I'm somewhat of a neophyte. I still carry my Franklin day planner—revolutionary at the time of its inception but a relic in my life and almost twenty-five years old. If I lost it … well, you don't want to witness that situation. It's a big black book, full of ragged pages, Wite-Out, and loads of stickers—labels, literally. So if you are in my address book and you've moved multiple times, there are labels upon labels on your designated plot. Maybe some Wite-Out. I joke that this day planner is an extension of my right arm. Clearly, I'm attached to this planner, and the "why" is beginning to make sense.

I received it when I worked for a corporation that insisted all of their employees have one. We had to sit through several hours of a training video to understand how we were to use it. You cannot imagine the torture this was for me. I was twenty-three. And the idea that I actually had any use for this "bible" was beyond me. Ironically, however, it turned out that this day planner/address book was something I could manage. Though I now have a MacBook, a scheduler on my iPhone, an iPad, and a pretty good brain, I cannot see myself making the transition into the cyber world. For some reason, my day planner seems safe. I think my organizational life would fall apart if I didn't have pen and paper to write my *"Call Dr. M. Get this from Lowe's. Don't forget dance at 4:00"*—is this possible on an iPad? Not for me! It is also, obviously, a little piece of my history ... and perhaps therein lies the attachment.

I've never lost this relic. People who are wizards at technology, who are deeply reliant on it and love it, surround me. I appreciate it but can't bring myself to depend on it. (I don't want to depend on anything! Yes, this is a character flaw.) I hate that feeling of fragmentation when something goes wrong with my phone or computer.

I've had many conversations with people around the changes in our culture that technology nurtures. Thank-you notes, books, newspapers, magazines, dictionaries, good old-fashioned encyclopedia sets, and address books—it depresses me that these things are disappearing, literally. We are losing touch with human contact—touch, literally. And what is happening with all of our other senses? I love the Kindle thing. Probably won't own one but appreciate its awesomeness. However, I love to walk through an airport and check out what people are reading. I love to sneak-read the book of the person sitting next to me on the airplane. I love the feel of a book in my hands. I love the smells of my books. I love looking at my books in all of my rooms, especially my daughter's, which has floor-to-ceiling shelves filled with books; one whole wall is children's stories, which will be there for all our time. And I worry very much about our contact with each other (people in general) and how it is evolving.

I feel the scars from my early death experiences led to my inability to maintain an address book. As you know, I didn't keep up with anyone from high school or college, except for Scott. I resist social networking—"resist" is putting it mildly. For me, it seems like a waste of time and energy and something about fraud. (This is undoubtedly a piece of the authenticity thing.) I don't Google people—that seems intrusive. Don't get me started on Twitter, though I can see its value in times of disaster.

I have enough intimacy in my job that I am overwhelmed at having more things to attend to, yet I wonder: is this about my unconscious grief? My many moves? If I associate my past relationships with the losses that occurred at the time, why would I want to "friend" those people? Wouldn't that only stir the pot of sadness I fought so hard to empty? Certainly, forming and maintaining attachments after so many losses became scary. Yet I needed relationships. I'm human, after all. I know I seek connections. Yes, the connecting of the dots.

Don't misunderstand: in my present life I have great, intimate, and dependable friendships that I will nurture and maintain for the rest of my life. But I'm sure that in my early years, my moving too fast made it impossible to sustain friendships, long term. I never had difficulty making new friends because I needed them. I am a bit of a social butterfly. And I was great about family—this was where I committed. I didn't need an address book for them; it was all in my head.

Ironically, I have kept the physical copy of every address book I've ever had. I have a dedicated drawer in my bedside table that houses all of them, though I don't visit them. Beginning with the first one, a classic teenager's diary, of sorts. In college, it became more professional, I liked to believe. Classic and black, not too complicated, it could fit in my back pocket—you can picture it. I'm sure they still carry them at Office Depot. When I was living in New York City, attempting a life as an actress, it was an artsy journal of sorts that I'd picked up in Chinatown. And not long after, I got the prized one I still carry today. Though it is beginning to fall apart, I'll deal with that crisis when it arrives. I believe I hold on to these books as a type of memoir—concrete evidence that I had a life. And there's something about time spent.

A year ago, I could explain away my lack of enthusiasm for e-mail, Facebook, and all other electronic communication in many intelligent manners yet, as you know, I'm now reexamining this resistance as a part of my grief reactions. I recently had to move forward with this idea of a "platform" for my book—a new "fancier" website, Facebook, Twitter, and a blog. I love the blog idea, as I get to write, but the whole platform scheme scared the daylight out of me. Not only as a therapist, but as a back-up singer. This is where I'm more comfortable behind the scenes. The only reason I ever had a website is because my friend was learning how to make them and offered to create one for me. I rarely went on it.

I was embarrassed at the idea of having one. Prior to my platform, I had been on Facebook only once, with a friend, to check out a man she was interested in. I was appalled. I couldn't believe how self-absorbed it all seemed. (I know I've probably just alienated all of my readers!) Now, I'm embracing this process as I'm trying to heal, understand myself, and be a part of the century in which I live. And admittedly, I've become quite the Facebook player!

Changes Your Address Book

Change (v.): to undergo a loss or modification of a position, course, or direction

Over the years, I've found myself saying to friends, family, and clients, "Grief changes your address book."

Though this was long before I understood how grief had dramatically affected my own "address book" and its content of contacts. When I made this remark, I wasn't making that connection consciously. The address book metaphor represented the second, unanticipated injury. (This includes the death of a marriage and divorce for children—oh! How that literally changes their address book.) The second wound isn't expected, and it adds another astonishing layer of hurt. The one where not only has your life been changed forever, but you are about to experience profound changes in your address book. There could be horrendous subtractions and breathtaking additions, and it will be mostly or completely unpredictable. And utterly disarming, in the "who would've guessed" sort of way.

This idea was solidified for me when my brother died, as I watched my parents grieve (my father and stepmother). As time unfolded for my family, the people who disappeared, or the ones who didn't know what to do, evidenced the second injury. And it changed their address book. People fell off the page. But there were new arrivals—people they knew casually who became intimate friends. Today, I'm sure my father would say there was a time when those with whom he did or didn't spend time was in direct relation to his grief experience—as I believe it is for most who experience profound loss.

This was true for me. When Scott was alive, he was close to a couple, Gary and Laura. Scott would often talk about them as if we all knew each other, but we did not. After Scott's death, they became my very close friends. We had adored and loved Scott and had that in common. And we are grateful for this connection, this unexpected blessing. I keep up with Scott's parents, too, and let them know how we are, because I need this connection to Scott.

As I became more conscious of my own grief experiences and their effects, I observed and worried about my kids, mostly my son. At his young age, he has witnessed way too much loss. We have a unique relationship and union in this way, though he doesn't know it yet. And he has absorbed his father's grief issues, which are mighty. My son's father lost his immediate family, terribly and unrelated, in an all-too-short period of time.

In our new town and on our street, two eighteen-year-old girls died, suddenly and tragically, within one year. I remember wondering how this was going to shape my children's future address books. I remember feeling scared about my daughter turning eighteen on that street. I know that's not fair or right, but I believe in the serendipity of things. I follow the map of synchronicity. I'm a notice-er. I immediately and somewhat consciously started thinking about moving off that street. We had moved to this new town, where a judge was shot by a sniper; the state controller was murdered by her husband; and *now this*. I also had a completely unavoidable car accident in which my car was hit three times. This was on the morning that my neighbor's daughter went missing, one of the eighteen-year-olds. It was too much. *I had to move.* And I had just moved from another state. And we were in one of the worst real estate markets ever! Didn't matter. I was post-traumatic stress disorder symptomatic, which means boy, was I anxious, and I began my search, though slow at first.

When we eventually moved into our new house, a house I'd fallen in love with (this *was* the prominent criterion), I told everyone, "Unless we leave the country or have some fantastic, irresistible opportunity somewhere else, we are never moving again!"

And I thanked God that I was living in a house that feels like my dream house. A dream because I feel safe in this house despite any conditions or circumstances in my life. I've joked that because the house is my age and therefore I couldn't have lived here before, I must have taken an arrow on the property in a past life—it is that familiar and comfortable.

At that point, when we purchased this house, and I decided to move in this economy, I still hadn't connected the grief dots. I only knew I was feeling traumatized by the events around me. And still today, when I experience an abandonment, I immediately think about places I could go—*leave*. And I notice the "for sale" signs all around me. I want to look into their houses.

Still, after all this awareness, the compulsion exists--at least I'm conscious about it.

The Leveling

Level (v.): to tear down, raze

Raze (v.): to destroy to the ground

Yes, I've known grief. And I believe I have mourned, though I am now questioning this. I won't be able to take off this new lens, this grief lens. The one that can change my address book. It's that unstoppable, heavy fog that envelopes you, and you can't escape. It is suffocating. You can't breathe. *You have no control.* I call this the "leveling." As I watched my parents experience this, I witnessed their inability to make it all okay after the unnatural, untimely death of a child.

They were normally skilled at making things okay, often much better than okay. My brother's death took them to a place they had not been. And they were in a social set where the unspeakable didn't happen. They were living the dream, and so were their friends. They were leaders in their community, movers and shakers, and undeniably happy. Don't get me wrong; this was not a problem-free world, but the problems were managed—well managed. They had control.

And then, the leveling. The thing about the leveling is there is nothing left to manage. It is the place after the tsunami. The devastation.

I believe when the unthinkable happens, the absurd can happen. We have these inane phrases like, "Everyone grieves in his own way." I guess that's true, yet our behavioral responses to grief are somewhat formulaic. It seems to me that we either know what it's like because we've been there and therefore, we know how to show up, or we've been raised well and have some sense of how to be present (show up). Or we have no idea what to do, but tradition has demonstrated that we, with good intentions, bring food or plants (more things to take care of, and there is no hunger—the leveling). Or the situation causes intense fear and anxiety, and we vanish.

Of course, all are responses to pain—our comfort levels with our own emotional pain and that of others. And we are not comfortable with emotional pain. So when we are leveled by excruciating emotional pain, all the eating, cleaning, drinking, humor, smoking, shopping, gambling, *moving*, and intellectualization—-all the busyness that was soothing in the past is not available to us. We are emotionally incapacitated. And it is universally unsettling.

It'd be nice if death came with a plan, like birth does. We are so prepared for the births of our children, down to the music we want playing—trying to control the outcome. We have no "death plan," of course. Not negating the legal trust stuff—most often this has nothing to do with music and blissful outcome. (Though both are protective.) I've often felt sickened by remarks like, "You should prepare yourself for ..."

For what? For the leveling, I suppose.

When I see this "prepare yourself" statement depicted on television or in the movies (knowing full well this statement is made in hospitals across the country on a regular basis), I wonder, who are we actually preparing? Are they essentially asking the leveled person to make it easier for the staff? After all, the more prepared *we* are, the less *they* have to deal with our stuff. No preparedness in the world will change the outcome of a tsunami. Yes, lives could be saved, but the aftermath would still be devastation.

Maybe we should hand out pencils to the ones who are grieving a death, like men with cigars at the birth of a child. Both are extraordinary events, but one may require the immediate ability to write down the name of someone or the quick use of an eraser. No ink. Things can change in an instant.

For those on the outside looking in, it may have seemed like I was leveled and grief-stricken following my double-whammy grief experience. After all, I cried for months when Scott died and still do when I think about him. I played certain songs repeatedly, built an altar, made collages, and indulged my pain and myself tremendously. I'm also pretty sure it was around this time that the "I gotta get out of here" seed was planted. The one that demonstrates the need for action, shift, and change. Leave my charmed and successful life in Napa. And it was very convincing. And compelling.

After all, any seed has the potential for beautiful abundant things.

The Living Lonely

Lonely (adj.): producing a feeling of bleakness or desolation

Most people who come to my psychotherapy practice with a grief issue think they should be "over it" within the first six months. They come in at the year mark—a magical juncture—thinking there is something wrong with them because they can't move past it. Yet there is no mention of the incredible loneliness they are experiencing. Only the self-criticism. The self-doubt.

Not too long ago, the book I was working on was titled *Grief Changes Your Address Book.* This idea had been churning around in my body and brain for a long time. During the process of working on this grief book, I met lots of people who had experienced the leveling. I was astonished. At first I thought I must be attracting this. I believe in the law of attraction—the idea that we can call things into our lives through conscious intention or unconscious inattention. One, very helpful; the other, not so great.

I started seeing the unspeakable death, the hidden mourning. I was having visions of women pushing their shopping carts, gliding up and down the aisles, silently nodding to each other. A nod that affirmed the belonging. The leveled place. The one you don't discuss. Where you live in secrecy. I would find myself at formal dinner parties seated next to the one person who had recently lost a child (most often an adult child, though that doesn't diminish the loss). I wondered, *Is this everywhere? Is this me?*

This experience has shown me how important it is to be open and sincere about what's happening in our lives because when I'd say, "I'm writing a book on grief," the doors would fly open in sync. *Wham!* Like the previews at the movie theatre—so loud and dramatic. Startling. And not at all what I expected—not so scary or depressing but profound and helpful. It is my contention that anything can be discussed when there is sincerity and kindness. These pieces connect us around ideas and wounds that we otherwise might be afraid to bring up. And of course, there is the greater piece: compassion.

One woman shared that after her son died, she was leveled for so many years, she thought she would never get over it. She said she felt so alone and came to believe there must be something wrong with her because of the amount of time. I can't tell you how many clients have said this to me in our first conversation, often on the initial phone call.

I remember a client who came in around the first anniversary of her father's death. She was in her mid-fifties. She was certain something was wrong with her because she missed him so much.

I explained to her, "Of course you miss him. You *lost* someone you've known your entire life. Someone you've *loved* your entire life. *Fifty-six years*. Every holiday. Every World Series. Every election. He was a part of your experiences. And you are supposed to be 'over it' at this juncture? How? You may never be over it."

It takes months of reconditioning through therapy for my clients to understand that it is normal to grieve for a number of years. *And I also mean, to be forever altered.* Validating this for my client was all she needed. After a short period, the veil lifted, and she could go on—still missing her father but knowing there was nothing wrong with that.

I tell my clients who are grieving, especially those who are leveled, "I don't believe 'time heals all wounds.' Time just puts distance between you and the acute pain of the actual event. But when we think about the actual event, for the rest of our lives, we will feel pain—and it will most likely be sharp. It *is* painful, and we won't collude with our culture of denial and 'move on.'"

This is what happens. We walk around with invisible veils. We have to "move on." Isn't that what we are told all of the time?

"Life goes on."

The problem is that nobody shares their loss anymore. Instead, we hear, "But he died a year ago, right?" We become forced to grieve in silence, in hiding, wearing our invisible veils. And our address book changes. The people who ask the "I don't get it"-type of questions become our past. It is even worse for those who believe they are supposed to be over it, because eventually, they begin to isolate even more, to hide the fact that they *aren't* over it. They truly are convinced they must be crazy. And the loneliness that is a naturally occurring piece of grief is heightened.

To me, the emptiness that grief creates becomes a specific type of loneliness. It creeps up and begins oozing out. And it needs, nurtures, and creates its own privacy. It's the filling up the holes in our hearts. Our loneliness—the missing of the loved one. How many times a day do we want to pick up the phone and call the person who is gone? How many times do we almost do this? It becomes unbearable when we feel like we can no longer share with someone. It's an emptiness. I still want to dish with Scott, this many years later. I can't believe he doesn't get to see *Paula Deen,* or *Top Chef,* or *Project Runway.* He would die over these *Housewives* shows. And the Food Network. Or Bravo. What fun we would be having.

It is the same with my brother, Doug. Even though I spent the last few years of his life wondering who he was, searching for the brother I once had, now I only miss the brother I knew. And there are many times when I want desperately to share something with him—and then the loneliness kicks in because I can't. I can't share it with him. Because he's gone. And I am left feeling lonely without him. Without them. Of course, I sometimes talk to both Scott and Doug as if they are looking down on me.

It is constant, my missing contacts. There are continual reminders— and we all have them, these absent loved ones. I *very rarely* mention my grief to anyone. I weep alone. I live in my own world around this. Again, it's a world that I'm sure is all around me.

The loneliness creates behaviors that can be troublesome. This is easily illustrated by overeating, yet I think all compulsive (addictive) behaviors have a piece of this. As I mentioned, my being an adult child of an alcoholic caused me to be hyper-vigilant so that I never experienced compulsivity. I think I *knew how* to binge when I was young, but as a youth, I saw it as "partying"—and it undoubtedly was—though I was still vigilant in my youth (and poked fun of for it). And there are those hormonal "retail therapy" days, followed by the "what was I thinking?" soon after. I'm sure I was soothing something.

When these behaviors get control of us, we end up more alone than ever, as we end up secretly soothing ourselves. And it can be very lonely. And very shaming. As I began examining my moving as a compulsive behavior (not so obvious, as it was not an annual experience), I discovered that my grief residue was lying in wait—like the dust you don't see on your tables until the afternoon sun hits it just right. And then it's alarming. And what you thought was clean is, in fact, very dirty.

And not so pretty.

Harold and Maude

Harold and Maude (n.): a 1971 American film that incorporates elements of dark humor and existentialist drama, with a plot that revolves around the exploits of a young man intrigued with death (from Wikipedia)[4]

Recently in our small town, a well-loved teenager died on our glorious mountain. It was heartrending, as it always is. Within a week, as I was leaving my downtown office, I saw cars everywhere. Then the familiar colors of the black-and-white vehicles and officers. Something was amiss. I felt instantly sick. I wondered if something was going on at the courthouse nearby, as there often is. The parking meters had hoods over them, so I surmised someone very important must have died, and this was the funeral. The governor? A senator? I don't read newspapers or watch the TV news, so this was quite possible, though I figured I would have heard it from other people if the governor had died.

Then, I thought about this teenager, this beloved boy, and I quickly did the math. He had died last Wednesday; this was Tuesday. Could this be *his* service? It was too soon, in my mind. It is always too soon in my mind.

I immediately went home, though I felt a compulsion to turn around and attend the service, to be with this family during their darkest moments. This was an unusual and unfamiliar urge on my part. This tragedy had moved me since the moment I heard about it. I attribute this to my own inner grief and to my love of teens. My desire to turn around was my need to be around grieving people. To be less alone in my own feelings of sadness; in my loneliness. Though I wouldn't attend a service that wasn't personal to me, I understand why people might do this. In the cult film *Harold and Maude*, Harold attends funerals of strangers regularly. He needs to be with others who share his state of mind. He's the perpetual mourner, the lonesome observer.

I went home and researched "death etiquette," wondering about the quickness of the funeral? Was there a rule on this? A law? Obviously, we have religious laws that dictate procedure for burials. And some of this is literally governed by our states. I find this preposterous. I believe if one of my kids were taken from me, you couldn't peel me off the floor to attend anything in a week's time. Yet we do it all of the time. We must. And the idea that there are laws about this ... I'm not a Libertarian but this gives me pause. I have a friend whose child died in another state but resided in this one. This produced all kinds of red-tape legal issues.

I have another friend whose two-year-old died suddenly, without warning. I was filled with admiration and bewilderment at the service *because they did such an incredible job.* The heart-wrenching and beautiful video of this child's short life—how did they manage? How on earth did they put it together in less than a week? How did anyone get off the floor? Out of bed?

I learned much in my quick research, and I found it interesting how quickly most formal religions dictate burial—within twenty-four hours. *Twenty-four hours!* This was a shock to me. How can anyone say good-bye to a loved one within twenty-four hours? I understand the autopsy rules. While some of my knowledge comes from *Law and Order*, I also have personal experience. My brother's case became a forensic investigation of sorts. Okay, fair enough when there are these types of questions. But death is personal and very private. And when there is trauma, it takes time to process. I found myself having thoughts about the entire process. For instance, 'if we are cremated or embalmed, what the heck does it matter, what's the big rush?' I know this is changing. New practices are emerging. I know we are having more celebrations of life, seasons after their loved one has died.

When my brother died, I did not go to see his body. It was a conscious choice. I knew that it was probably better for me, as a part of the grieving process, to see him, but I *just couldn't*. Now, I think I probably should have. I was still reeling from my best friend Scott's loss, and I had no strength left in me. I was in shock and the only clear thought I had was that the vision of him would be the end of me. I didn't want to remember him lifeless, on a slab. I didn't want that picture in my head. Yet as a result, I didn't get to say good-bye. At the time, I felt so angry and hurt, I thought, *What is the point? I won't be saying good-bye. I'll just be saying what I have said to him since we were kids: "What the hell? What have you done now?"*

As it is with death by overdose, I was robbed of the experience of loving and comforting my brother in the end, as one normally does when a loved one is dying from a disease. There was no stroking, no shared intimate, end-of-life, moments. No professed love. Just exhaustion from the tiresome work and relentless fear. Anyone who has a loved one with an addiction or mental illness knows this experience. And when they leave us, we are left with inexplicable pain. And in defense, this bloats into anger in an effort to avoid the suffering.

As my family and I were leveled and true to our feelings, we planned nothing in terms of a service. We had nothing in us. One of my best friends, a pastor, urged me to put something together for my brother's friends and community. She gently explained what I knew to be true—that it is an important step in the grieving and mourning process. My parents were hesitant to attend—they were still on the floor. In the end, we were all present and stumbled through it. It was probably within two weeks of his death, though that doesn't seem possible. We held a service that celebrated his life. My friend took care of all the arrangements. The church seemed filled, and there were a lot of women stepping forward to testify to my brother's charms and attractiveness. This amused us to no end and was wholly healing. Seven months later, we celebrated his life in another family gathering, believing we would spread his ashes in Lake Tahoe on his birthday. That didn't happen. Seven months later, it was too soon. Now, almost ten years later, it is too soon. And I still haven't said good-bye.

When Scott died, there was a wake the night before the funeral, and I didn't want to go. The very idea was unbearable for me. I'd heard there would be an open casket. In my life, I had never been to any type of a wake. I think my husband held me throughout the wake. He kept me upright. I remember it vividly—Scott's body in the casket. How he wasn't in his body. How strange he looked. I studied his form. I found myself pondering the practice of embalming. This all was new to me. I wanted to touch him. Poke him, his rubbery form. I stuck to the science (seeing the embalming process like a preservative); I was practiced at this. It's a good way to avoid feelings, think of the absolutes. I thought Scott was likely laughing hysterically from above. He was pretty vain and might have had something to say about how he looked—something funny and twisted. He had a wicked sense of humor.

These ideas made me feel a little bit better—a very little. My favorite uncle's flower arrangement was near enough to the casket that I found myself contemplating the array of flowers, counting the petals. Again, math. I was trying to stay in my head. My body wasn't available. The fact that my uncle's family had sent these moved me deeply, as they, too, loved Scott and grieved his loss, all the way from another coast.

In my mind, there were hundreds of people at Scott's funeral, and it was a sight! (Scott loved spectacle, so I hope he was there to see it.) I'm sure not everyone knew his charms and attractiveness personally, yet I have no doubt the attendance was a great comfort to his parents. Scott is buried in his home state of Kentucky; this is what he wanted. It is definitely what his family needed. In my mind, however, it was all so fast. And surreal. And of course, I want him here, with me. But I'm glad he's home. And someday I'll visit him at his gravesite. When I'm ready.

When my mom died, I have foggy memories of a service in Michigan, where there was no body, no urn, no representation of her at all, in my mind. I remember wondering, "What are we doing here?"

I couldn't tell you the location. My memories are hazy: a room, not a church; no one familiar, though some too familiar (for an embarrassed teen). I wanted to disappear. And I did. I spent the summer on Nantucket as a nanny. And in July of that summer, at my mother's family crypt in Vermont, there was a service in the graveyard. My mother came from a long and prestigious line of Vermonters named Proctor, so there were many local attendees, although my memory could be cloudy. I knew very few of them from her side; a lot from my father's side. My father's family all came, though they hadn't been in my mother's life for some time. They were present, for me and for her. In my mind, it was maddening to see how few immediate family from her side did not attend. For instance, I was her only child there, the good and dutiful daughter. And I believe her half brother's were absent.

Again, there was no headstone. Nothing corporeal. This bothered me to no end. My aunt explained there were some difficulties about making it happen. Though I believe we leave our bodies even before our last breath, I like the physical representation—something to talk to, to see. Something symbolic. And I haven't been back since.

When my mother-in-law died, her daughter split her ashes and divided them into five urns. One for each of her kids. As it arrived in the mail, we didn't know what to think. I had never seen this practice. I thought it was strange at the time, yet so thoughtful. My husband kisses his "mom" hello every morning. I am so glad my sister-in-law did this. We need a physical connection to our lost loved ones. I guess this is why I have my altars. I've done one for each loved one who passed. After some time, I put the altars away in a safe place.

DABDA

DABDA (n.): an acronym for the five stages of grief

As a therapist, I read books that are highly recommended. Books by smart people. And lots of books by New Thought authors. Books that endorse my beliefs in metaphysics. And in self-help.

As a therapist in denial, I refer, sometimes too soon, some of these grief books to my clients. I say "too soon," as I remember recommending Pema Chodron's *When Things Fall Apart* to a client who was grieving. Not a good thing at the time. I was surprised by her reaction, after all, aren't I a fabulous therapist? I picked up the book again, though I know it well. The inside flap, which I'm pretty sure is as far as my client got, read:

"There is a fundamental opportunity for happiness right within our reach, yet we usually miss it—ironically, while we are caught up in attempts to escape pain and suffering." [5]

No wonders there.

I remember that someone sent my parents a copy of this book after my brother died. I have no doubt it was put away for a sunny day. There were too many rainy days ahead. Recently, my friend's father died. I told her not to let her mom read grief books for at least a year. The heart and the brain are temporarily haywire. In time, the rewiring of the brain will take place, and books will be received. And able to be read. I read *The Year of Magical Thinking* by Joan Didion when it was released. I couldn't tell you what it was about. I was still numb from my own loss. Many years later, I reread her book and found it wholly helpful.

Swiss-born psychiatrist Elisabeth Kübler-Ross developed the five stages of grief in her now famous book, *On Death and Dying*, in 1969. The stages have been abbreviated as DABDA[6] and stand for:

- D—Denial
- A—Anger
- B—Bargaining
- D—Depression
- A—Acceptance

I explain to my clients that the stages are not necessarily in this order; maybe they are the opposite. Maybe we are stuck in one and have skipped completely over another. But I think Kübler-Ross has provided an incredibly wise resource. This acronym and research was derived from her work with terminally ill patients and originally was meant for those managing the dying process. It has since expanded in its usage.

Today, we also use the stages of grief for those left behind—the living grievers, instead of the loved ones who are leaving. Clearly, I was stuck in denial and had some issues with anger. Believe it or not, many are barely in touch with their anger. My parents haven't demonstrated any anger toward my brother (to my knowledge), while I stayed furious for a long time.

Following my mom's death, surely I was in denial. Yet as an adolescent, this played out differently, developmentally. Again, I played hard and felt numb a lot, though I was determined to have a good time. Eventually, I felt angry. I remember, early on, having angry thoughts but quickly suppressed them, as a good and dutiful daughter would. After all, my mom died. I would allow myself only to feel sorry for her, not examine the fact that her children—that I—suffered in the process. That I was abandoned even long before she died. A mother who secretly drinks and is addicted to alcohol must be abandoning her children on a regular basis. This I know. I can remember sitting on our green shag carpet, while my parents were in their recliners. I was poised perfectly next to my mom, who was holding her scotch on the rocks. I was like a loyal puppy, waiting for any sign of admiration, affection, or even existence.

Looking back at my early twenties, I now believe I had a form of depression—not clinical but agitated. The kind that keeps you moving too fast. The kind that reinforces the denial. The kind that goes unnoticed because you're busy achieving things. My accomplishments certainly disguised any pain I may have been experiencing.

Most people get stuck in wondering about the bargaining aspect—or as I call it, the betrayal. The bargaining part of the DABDA acronym mostly comes up in our relationship with God. When bad things happen, we start skipping our Sunday service when we need it most. We start to question, "*WHY?* Why did you let this happen?"

Or we ask philosophically, "Do you really exist? Do I actually need you? What good are you?"

When we lose someone we love deeply, we start the bargaining with God—almost in a dream state or delusional: "God, if you turn back time, I'll start going to church. I'll never _____ again!"

We want desperately to change the circumstance. To go back. To change time. To bargain—the price, the date, what we said, what we did, what we didn't say, what we didn't do. After all, the price is unreasonable, incomprehensible, and unlivable.

I sometimes explain using my personal experiences—a therapist no-no; we are not meant to have personal experiences—by saying, "We bargain with God because there was a betrayal. My brother betrayed me when he relapsed and died." And I think but do not say aloud, *Alone, in a hotel room.* And in remembering Scott's ravaged body, I add, "My best friend's body betrayed him when he got cancer."

I believe in grief work—this bargaining piece is critical. Well, maybe all of Kübler-Ross's stages need to be worked through, but the bargaining is tricky … because of the betrayal. These pieces can be tightly locked away in our psyche, as they represent the most painful parts. After all, how can we be angry with the dead? How can we feel betrayed by them? It just doesn't seem fair. And we don't believe it'll change anything, especially the loneliness—which, ironically, is where God is very handy. We are never truly alone when we feel connected to something greater.

When my best friend, Scott, was diagnosed with cancer, I was happily involved with a metaphysical church. I took classes, served on committees, and attended regularly with my son. I had community. As soon as Scott died, I stopped going. I felt so alone that I couldn't bear to be in the presence of others, especially in such an intimate setting. A year and a half later, after my brother died, my church community showed up at my door. They hadn't seen me in a long time but got word of what was happening and brought me food, love, and support. I remember being so surprised and moved by this. Yet I still struggled with the intimacy of it, after the loss. And my attendance at church was never the same.

I was alone. And I undoubtedly felt betrayed by my beliefs.

It's PTSD, Not ADHD, OCD, ADD, or OCCD

Not (adj.): used as a function word to make negative a group of words

I made up OCCD. It stands for obsessive-compulsive cyber disorder. But that's another book. And maybe that's the *'negative in a group of words.'* The thing about my interpretation of post-traumatic stress disorder, or PTSD, is that it is loose. As you know, I have worn a trauma lens. I explain this to my clients by saying that most people hear the acronym PTSD and think of Vietnam veterans; this is when it first became acknowledged as a psychiatric disorder. I suppose this recognition is natural. People assume it's a disorder for veterans of war, but there are many other circumstances which produce post traumatic stress. I use an even broader lens when there is anxiety following trauma and how we define it.

Today, tragically, PTSD is rampant, after our involvements in Afghanistan and Iraq. And we are not giving enough attention to this epidemic. I, myself, fell victim to this collusion. A couple of years ago, because of my spiritual practice, I gave up watching the news. I wanted my reality to be my own, not created for me by "talking heads." Yet I feel guilty about the fact that this means ignoring the extreme difficulties these wars have produced. When I find myself near a television that has on the 24 hour news cycle on, I'm taken aback by how little this gets addressed in the media and what is considered news. Meanwhile, these families' serious stories of struggle are waiting to be told. The statistics on suicides of servicemen is staggering. Consequently, these families are left more alone and less supported than ever.

If you look back at the American Psychiatric Association's DSM-IV (Diagnostic and Statistical Manual)[7] criterion for post-traumatic stress disorder, it is very specific and includes *"experiencing, witnessing, or confronting an event that involves actual or threatened death or injury, or a threat to the physical integrity of oneself or others, with an immediate reaction of intense fear, helplessness, or horror."* I attended a lecture in grad school where the professor laid out the symptoms for PTSD, juxtaposed with the experiences of a child raised by an alcoholic—and they were identical. Hence, a child raised by an alcoholic could suffer from PTSD. If a therapist sticks to a strict diagnostic interpretation of the disorder, however, I believe this diagnosis can be missed.

I have seen many clients who are PTSD symptomatic and have not been diagnosed, though they've seen many therapists. It is easily lost because of the strict interpretations, I believe. For me, diagnosing is not critical (and can be detrimental in this age of health care), but recognizing and treating the symptoms is critical. It's particularly helpful for clients with PTSD to know they have it. It provides relief and an explanation for why they feel the way they do.

In my practice, I offer to my clients my elementary yet (I believe) supportive explanation of how trauma works on the body. I describe how trauma enters the body on a cellular level. Cells have memory. Trauma induces an adrenaline response. This can feel good and certainly powerful but ultimately, it's harmful. It's a physiological, primitive response—the fight or flight. And adrenaline ends up craving its own response. Think of the adrenaline junkies you have known. First responders (police, fire fighters, ER staff, therapists) obviously are susceptible to this seduction. That's why most of us enter these professions. We already have layers upon layers of trauma in our bodies. I'm pretty certain you could interview most thrill-seekers and find a traumatic event in their past.

Many modalities—brief modalities—treat the symptoms of PTSD quite successfully, without talk therapy. These are very helpful when used adjunctively with psychotherapy. Long after attending graduate school, long after specializing in PTSD, I observed my own PTSD symptoms when Scott was dying of cancer and thereafter. It was the first time I was on the outside looking in. It was remarkable and so different from past events that caused these feelings, when I didn't understand what was happening. I could finally experience firsthand how these symptoms operated *consciously*. I didn't like it, but it wasn't wreaking havoc in my life as it could have been—as it does for so many others—purely because I had the knowledge. And I've been aware ever since. And so has my husband. I had to explain it to him: PTSD can make us feel like crazy people—looking to control, feeling frightened of fallout, an unsettling feeling in the pits of our stomachs at the sound of fire engines or the sight of weapons.

The anxiety alone caused me to behave in ways my husband needed to understand. For instance, when I am symptomatic, I need him to check the doors at night—or convince me that he did. When I'm not experiencing symptoms, I trust that this is done. Or I'm not so concerned about it. I know that it's all going to be okay. I'm simply a more relaxed person. Also, when I am symptomatic, I am jumpy—so don't sneak up on me! Now that I'm conscious of these things, they don't run my life (or his) and haven't for a long time. But there are those times when I feel a little trigger. And I'm less calm. I share with my clients (when appropriate) that I have PTSD, but it's in remission—today.

However, if I were to have a car accident on the way home, all bets are off.

Ahhhh, the Adrenaline

Epinephrine, also known as adrenaline (n.): a hormone *and* neurotransmitter. *It increases heart rate, constricts blood vessels, dilates air passages and participates in the* fight-or-flight response *of the* sympathetic nervous system[8]

When I searched for a definition for adrenaline, this is what I found. I was trying to stay within my sources, my Webster and Wikipedia. Adrenaline or epinephrine is powerful stuff. And presents different in children, and is therefore tricky. I've walked the halls of many elementary schools where there would be that one child, sitting on a chair outside of the classroom, *every day.* I'd march to the principal's office, demanding to know why he (yes, it was usually a boy) was out in the hall on a regular basis. Surely there was a better solution. These were the kids I loved to observe, loved to advocate for, because they needed me. They needed someone to explain that there are other disorders besides attention deficit hyperactivity disorder (ADHD, very popular beginning in the mid-'80s) and bipolar disorder (popularity, the mid-'90s) that could contribute to their behavior. A child with any trauma experience could easily look like a child with ADHD. And putting them in the hall every day would only add to their already complex picture.

Naturally, the school administrators were certain there was no trauma. I can't blame them. Nobody wants to think about this with regard to children; it's sickening. And yet I'm constantly amazed and surprised by what one considers traumatic. I remember interviewing a mom about her anxious child and searching for when and where the trauma occurred. The mom was clear: her life didn't involve any trauma. I sought harder. And harder. And even harder. Eventually, I found out the family had been in a violent car accident, and all four family members ended up in the hospital. (They obviously wanted to forget about it. And had done so.)

Well, anyone who has been in a mild or violent car accident knows the feeling of that adrenaline pumping through your body and how sick yet exhilarating it can feel. Even the flashing red lights in your rearview mirror create quite the adrenaline response. Now, mind you, I'm sure some experts would debate successfully my lack of science in this explanation, but this is my spiel for my clients. They have found it helpful and understandable, which is fundamental to my work. (I have also completely ignored the locus coeruleus, which is a small area in the brain stem containing norepinephrine neurons. This is considered the central place in the brain for anxiety and fear. There is plenty to read on the brain and anxiety, if you so desire.)

In treatment, it's critical that the therapist and client understand the adrenaline response. Once the client's able to recognize the physiology, there's room for great change. For instance, prior to ever seeing a therapist, an adult could hear about a contained fire down the street in his neighborhood. This creates anxiety, as this person's house burned down when he was three. In an effort to get away (and get information), the man drives down the street and consequently smells the smoke. This produces an adrenaline response. Now the man feels exhilarated and anxious. Perhaps he will go to a bar to "get away" and drink too much, to calm his nerves. Perhaps he'll head to a buffet to stuff his feelings.

After seeing a therapist, this person will be able to recognize the initial trigger—the fire and the smell, followed by the anxiety; and how the need to see the evidence (a trauma response) triggers more symptoms (olfactory response—a three year old would remember smells more than images). After figuring this out in therapy, this person will learn other ways to cope that are most likely healthier than the ones used previously; he'd learn a different behavioral response.

The adrenaline response is what we recognize more than the obvious other cues. Our bodies tell us something is affecting us negatively. Since adrenaline can feel powerful, however, we can ignore it, *like it*, and be unconscious of it, and then bad things can happen—things like too many roller coaster rides, watching scary horror flicks, jumping off cliffs into quarries, or three-day concerts with hallucinogens. In my early twenties, these were my drugs of choice.

A Margarita on the Beach

On (prep.): used as a function word to indicate means or agency, reduplication, or succession in a series

PTSD symptoms can create chaos. After all, the trauma induces an adrenaline response that kicks in and makes us feel like we can conquer the world. I spent an entire decade conquering five states and three countries. Early on, this involved roller coasters, scary horror flicks—anything for the adrenaline, by any means or agency. Anything to support the denial. Including men. As a young adult, most of my relationships (friendships and romantic) involved a powerful, unconscious connection constellated in the arena of post-traumatic stress and codependency. I was attracted to rescuers because I needed rescuing. These are potent forces. Without conscious awareness, I could attract this purely because of my circumstances and these conditions—the old "moth to a flame."

Think of the alcoholic who enters the room with four hundred strangers and finds the few other alcoholics immediately and hangs out with them. These human chemistries/energies are magnetic. In graduate school, I was in a small-group process class where I experienced these energies (you might want to avoid these). On the very first night, the woman next to me announced she was uncomfortable with me. It was something about the way I reminded her of her daughter. The professor asked me how it made me feel. I replied, "I don't know. I think she must come from an alcoholic family system. She doesn't know me, so she's plugging into something else."

I don't think my comment was well received by the woman, but my professor agreed with my assessment. We explored each other's stories, and it was true. She actually reminded me of my mom. And as it turned out, she was a recovering alcoholic.

Early on, and most often, I didn't see these connections coming. I never understood them. It would feel like I'd met my soul mate, like something "otherly" was operating. Well, there was, just not so romantic. Don't get me wrong; I believe in otherly connections but for me, as an adult child of an alcoholic with powerful grief issues, my training and intuition have forced me to acknowledge other past causal circumstances. And I do consider myself to be open to anything. I am a firm believer that *there is no such thing as coincidence.*

Sadly and regretfully (oh, how I hate to say that), my romantic relationships would not last. I would get bored as soon as we were committed, as soon as the intimacy and love became real. Intimacy is a real buzz-kill to an adrenaline junkie. Why would I want to commit to someone when I could be sitting on a beach with a margarita and my latest rescuer, waiting for our parasail ride? The very idea that someone could love me was agitating. And so I would move. Literally. *Until I did my work,* I was often too codependent to break up with someone. These were very good guys, and I didn't want to hurt them, so I would transfer programs or find jobs out of state. I even went so far as to attend a special training across the Atlantic—*twice.* The funny thing is, I am a monogamous person. I enjoyed playing house. I lived with my boyfriends pretty quickly after we were together. This bothers me about my then self—that I didn't take this seriously, though I'm sure I thought I did at the time. Clearly, I couldn't tolerate it after a point. Probably after reality set in with the depth of the feelings.

The final blow, the one that changed everything, was when I left one good man for another (I had never done that before), married him, and had a child. That was reckless, and I went into therapy right after our divorce—and to graduate school in clinical psychology.

I'd love to say I have no regrets. Hah! That's a good one. Makes me giggle (and cringe) when I hear people say this. Ironically, and easily explained through psychology, as I began my journey of recovering (or remission, I should say) from the PTSD, I stepped into the rescuer role. This was when my real work began—my ACoA work.

Ugh, Regret

Regret (n.): a grief or pain tinged with emotion (as disappointment, longing, or remorse) and distress

Yes, I find it somewhat amusing when someone says, "I have no regrets."

And I secretly think, *bulls**t*. Regret is a part of life. It doesn't mean we would do it differently, but of course we have regret. I regret not handling my moving with a little more consciousness. Or with a little more honesty and integrity. I did the best I could at the time. And the best I could do was *run*. (Have I said I was moving too fast?)

Regret is an important and devastating aspect of losses associated with death. Personally, my death regrets come when I consider how I spent my time. I wish—and I'm certain I'm not alone in this—that I had spent more time with the ones I've lost. Now I know this is natural; the time is gone. How could I not regret the time lost? And like all regrets, we can rationalize and intellectualize this to kingdom come. That's the point. Regret doesn't mean we could or would have done it differently. I couldn't travel across country as a working single parent in graduate school to see my grandmother, who was in a nursing home thirty miles off the East Coast, all the while trying to manage my brother's addiction. Still, I regret not having seen her. Not saying good-bye.

I really regret not seeing more of Scott when he was ill. To have any more seconds, minutes, hours … anything. Again, I was a busy single parent with a hectic lifestyle who was in complete denial of what was happening. And I loved him very much. (And I miss him every moment of every television day!)

This death regret leads to defense. The "I have no regrets" comment is just a big linebacker. It's protective. It guards us, but eventually, in my case, it came out in the form of verbal vomit. It went like this: first off, Scott was gay, so I had to immediately defend him by saying, "It was colon cancer, not HIV!" Then, he was my very best friend, not a woman but a gay man. I would emphasize, "We were like Will and Grace *but closer*! He was my first phone call, godfather to my son, and my daughter is named after him. We practically lived together in Ohio, New York City, and California!"

Inside, I was protesting, pleading, "Do you understand?"!

I needed to provide evidence that this was a huge loss. I didn't believe anyone understood the depth of my anguish. No reassurance in the world would satisfy me. This, of course, is a natural part of mourning. And it made me feel better about my relentless regrets. (And now I've put it in print—further validating and defending our relationship.)

Regret can also cause reaction. The grief regret can especially do this. I see this all the time. Personally, my most recent experience involved the death of my mother-in-law, who was a great lady. It was sudden and related to hospital error—there was a mis-management of the hospital monitors. There was bedlam. My sister-in-law, who was closest to my mother-in-law, emotionally and physically, lived in small-town New Hampshire. She immediately went into PTSD mode after her mother's death, gearing up for a lawsuit in an effort to avoid the pain she was feeling—and we all encouraged this.

"Somebody has to pay."

Her mom was her first morning phone call and her end of the day. The void created by this loss was intolerable. The process of trying to figure out what happened was daunting. And she didn't have much help. Eventually, she gave up trying. This sister-in-law also was the only one *not* at her mom's bedside when she died. I've often wondered if she regretted that decision. I believe at the time, it was best. It was far too painful for her, obviously, because she would have been there otherwise. There is no manual for this. Yet she may feel this specific emotion and have no place to put it, because she *wouldn't* have done it differently.

Ugh, regret sucks.

Oh-So-Perfect Perception

Perception (n.): quick, acute, and intuitive cognition interpreted in the light of experience

Trauma changes our perceptions of reality. For example, a child comes home and finds Dad passed out (from drinking) and in an unusual position—half off the couch. The child has an immediate fear response: Is Dad alive? Is something awful going to happen? Even preverbal children feel this. Mom comes in and explains that Dad is "just sleeping." The child learns he cannot trust his own feelings or perception of reality.

I had a strong feeling in high school that my mom was going to die. It made me feel like a drama queen, and I was treated as such by my dad. He didn't mean to treat me like a drama queen but he would say things like, "Alcoholics live to be very old; look at your grandfather." He didn't want me to worry so much, and he didn't know the different characteristics of male and female alcoholics. Women die much younger from this disease. Every time I heard an ambulance in middle school, I was sure they were driving to my house. Everyone around me poked holes in my perception. My fears were unfounded—until she died, three weeks before my high school graduation.

This perception thing has played out differently, both culturally and socially, over the last hundred years or so as we change how we grieve. At one time, we wore black for a year (and women wore a veil). We had rituals that allowed for more time and direct experience (I'm picturing Scarlett O'Hara's mother's dead body laid out on the dining room table.) We had perfect perception of what was happening. And we allowed for it. Now, we live in a society that encourages us to move on. Our perception is that we are not okay when we are grieving, when we are leveled. And consequently, the result is that the leveling isn't real. And yet we are in our most vulnerable state.

I think most people's perception of grief is convoluted, but that seems natural. Another misperception. We know the definition of grief. We kind of know how it looks. We can recall various movies with great grief scenes at bedsides—*the woman drops to her knees, wailing, "No, no!" with arms at her side for the camera's full view of her torn face. The angry father paces in the background, fists tightly clenched, and grunts, "I'll get the bastard who did this!"*—and this confuses our initiation into the process of grief.

When I ask clients about what it means to grieve, I get a response as if I'd asked what it means to cry. It is a weakness. Grieving means crying? We know crying isn't necessarily about grieving. And then there is the usual cliché, *"everyone grieves in their own way."* Yet we know from most books, movies, and pop culture that it is a process, one that involves crying, if we let it. I've been a great and consistent crier—for others. I've believed in utilizing my tear ducts since I was young—we have them for a reason. Yet I now know that I didn't fully grieve my own losses. I didn't seek therapy at the time of my double loss. I had to push on. Move forward. Get over it. I had no time for therapy. I'm sure this was an avoidance of pain, the emotional pain I was running from. After all, I know better; I'm not afraid to seek help. I consider myself courageous. So, why then, in the midst of such life-shattering events, did I avoid what I know to be helpful? This, remember, was when I dropped out of my spiritual routine as well.

If someone were to have asked me what it means to grieve, I think I would have said, "It's a process not easily defined but involves intermittent and violent waves of excruciating pain, followed by extreme forms and intense periods of avoidance." Yet in my practice, I see and hear that it's perceived as a weakness. I can't get on board with this, so I gently poke holes in this idea. No matter what we believe, we are grieving, especially when we've been leveled. The leveling lets us know we are grieving. The disorientation, the incapacitation is happening, and evident no matter what. And I did cry a whole heck of a lot in my midthirties. But that was kind of all I did. (Oh, and got married and had a baby. Just a little distraction.) And then I crossed another state line.

From Wall Street or Main Street to Speaker Street

From (prep.): a place where a physical movement begins

Grief can completely alter the course of your life, as can trauma in much the same way. We see this all the time with foundations, organizations, and movements. Most motivational speakers have endured a harrowing experience that changed everything. And quite possibly changed their address books. From Main Street or Wall Street to Speaker Street. Sometimes literally, their life takes on a whole new direction. And their mission becomes practically a physical representation of their loss or their loved one. A memorial, of a life. A life that will be sorely missed. This platform represents what could have been. And what was. In my case, grief literally altered the direction of my life. I can see this clearly. I could create a diagram: on the left, grief and/ or trauma event; on the top, locales. At each intersection, dates.

My father and stepmother put together an intimate and stunning shade pavilion in my brother's name as a memorial. At first, it made me feel awkward, uncomfortable. After all, he didn't win a peace prize; he overdosed on drugs. But he was a good person. And a good son. And they needed to do something—something that would ease the excruciating pain they were experiencing at their loss. It turned out to be a wonderful project (and it won awards in the architectural world). I love the pavilion, especially the fact that as my father was leveled, he built something— literally. And that something, the pavilion, raised him up. It is beautiful as my brother was. (If you are ever driving through Nevada on Interstate 80, just east of Reno/Sparks, it is off the Patrick Road exit 28, to the right, on the Truckee River. Same exit as the infamous Mustang Ranch.)

What I find disheartening—and sometimes alarming—is the misplaced and sometimes malicious guidance to which the grieving can fall victim during these vulnerable times, especially when they are in the loneliest aspect of grief; when they are leveled. I think this is most visible in the celebrity community. Their lives are already surrounded by possible vultures who seemingly were doves prior to their tragedy, and now that they are in a state of weakness, anything goes. All of a sudden they are, as any of us could, making decisions that take them from Sunset Boulevard to a physician's office on Rodeo Drive. Or even worse. And what should be so very personal and private becomes so disgustingly public.

I delivered a eulogy and sang a favorite song at both my brother's and Scott's services. I wish someone would have advised me to just sit and observe, to mourn. Not that I would have listened. I was so wrapped up in my grief, I had to "perform." I look back at this with embarrassment, even though I know it was a part of my process. My wail. I still think about protection during that time—or the lack thereof.

Another example of the vulnerability of grief, though mostly invisible, is in the elderly community, where bereavement is ever present. While they are mourning, there is the potential for fiduciary, emotional, and even physical abuse, most often by their own adult children. We see this depicted on television and yet, it is very much a reality. I find these particular cases disgusting and disheartening. After all, we can all imagine growing old some day. I wonder about our culture's attitude toward's our elderly and how very different it is in other places.

I find these instances, both the invisible and the visible, particularly egregious as managers, lawyers, and guardians; hired to act in their best interest, surround them. Yet no one is offering real protection. No one is telling them "just be." Instead, there is collusion. The old react collusion. No one is saying, "Slow down. Don't make any decisions right now. Take a break. Maybe head to Main Street, USA, for a while." I hear they have lovely soda fountains.

Harry's Generation

Generation (n.): a group of individuals having contemporaneously a status which each one holds only for a limited period

I remember the morning of Sept. 11, 2001, like it was yesterday. I'm sure we all do. Providentially, I watched the whole tragedy unfold on live television as Scott was in the midst of chemo and up at all hours. Otherwise, we would never have seen it as it was happening. We were on the West Coast. It was our time together, the early hours, watching morning shows while on the phone. Looking back, I was already in some sort of a dream state, going through this dying process with Scott. Obviously, that morning, the situation was unreal. I remember being grateful because I could alert my family quickly, as my sister lived in New York City. After having lived through the earthquake in San Francisco in 1989, I knew how quickly communication might collapse.

In a daze, I automatically went to my office, pretty early, feeling like the walking wounded. This was only two hours after the second tower collapsed.

I bumped into my landlord and officemate, a female attorney, who said, "I'm just thinking about the kids, the soldiers."

I was baffled. "What do you mean?"

We were both in shock.

"We'll be going to war immediately," she said.

I was stunned. Why did she think this? What did she know? (The look on my face was the kind that fuels the Botox industry today.)

I actually thought she'd come to a bizarre conclusion—certainly a rush to judgment. I remember thinking of all those souls transitioning at once. So incredibly tragic. And of the mass amounts of PTSD our country now had a responsibility to assist as we were all traumatized. It was unimaginable.

My female attorney landlord officemate was right. We reacted quickly.

Instead of acknowledging and addressing the mass amounts of anxiety and depression we now had, as a nation and a world, we colluded with our allies and made it all much, much worse. I remember watching Congress, voting on our decision to go to war. I stared at their faces—as best I could. I could see the shock. It was glaring. Seeing their faces was like looking in the mirror. I couldn't believe how quickly this came together. How could they be meeting when we, as a nation, were leveled, when we were on the floor? I suppose they thought it was their duty to get up off the floor. Ultimately, they may have been sitting in chairs, but to me they looked like sheets. As we all did. White sheets. No structure. No real form. And easily blown away. Not a good time to be making big decisions.

September 11, 2001, Afghanistan, Iraq, and now, the economy—these are the events that have shaped and defined a generation of kids in our country. I think about this often when I'm working with teens and young adults—what it must be like for them. Beyond what difficulties brought them to me in the first place, there is this broad and grave overlay. And a whole lot of grief. Or trauma.

It is also the generation that has the opportunity to engage and embrace (nice way of saying "become addicted to") violent video games. And they do. I'm shocked at the young ones in my office playing these games with their fathers. And last but not least, they are the generation that grew up with *Harry Potter*—an extraordinary and very dark story. I worry about these babes, my son included, and how this will manifest.

I watched the immediate news coverage of Osama bin Laden's killing. I was captivated—I'd given up news as a part of my spiritual diet, but I'd been looking for *Desperate Housewives* when the report came on. This was an unexpected fix. I stayed up into the wee hours, watching. I was amazed by the young people celebrating in front of the White House and at Ground Zero. I'd worked with and thought about this generation for years. This Y generation. During that evening, watching CNN's coverage of that remarkable event—I was mostly captivated by the actions of the Navy SEALs; *amazing*. I kept thinking about those young people, partying. What was this? An excuse to get crazy? Patriotism? I wondered what the firefighters were thinking, as they sat soberly watching them.

In the days following, I asked the teens and twenty-somethings I know close to me, "what did you think about the capture of Bin Ladin?" They simply didn't feel like it was a big deal. I attribute this to their unfortunate history. In their young years, times have been terribly negative. They've learned to not take things too seriously. Remember, this is also the generation that has fueled reality television in the United States. They've had to develop a sense of complacency. It's good for covering up the anxiety. They don't get excited about much in the real world—I'm generalizing, of course. I see it all the time. I've found it fairly (and sadly) typical that this momentous event wasn't discussed in their school. This always bothers me.

Scott died in 2002; my brother in 2003. I remarried in 2003. My daughter was born in January 2005. Busy times, full of reaction. And my family and I left our charmed life in Napa, California in the middle of 2006.

.

Securing a Sibling

Securing (v.): act to make safe against adverse contingencies

L ots of children are born into grief. Born out of grief. A woman sends her man off to war with a baby in her belly, mourning the loss of the experience of being together, while anticipating a joyous and potentially bittersweet experience. My sister was born just before my father was shipped off in 1960. I often wonder what that was like for all of them. I was born a month after John F. Kennedy was murdered. I can't imagine what this was like for my mom and dad, for the country. As parents, we naturally worry about the world into which we are bringing our children. Or we should. I wonder about how current events will impact my children's life.

As you may have deduced, my own children were born among grief. My son's father had lost his sister and mother in previous years, before we were married, due to independent circumstances. Four days after we told my father-in-law that we were pregnant, he had a heart attack and died. I believe, after all the loss in his life, our news somehow gave him permission to move on, to find peace. My son provided his dad with a family after he had lost one. I am grateful for this. My son also was quite attached to his godfather, Scott, and his uncle Doug. He endured a lot of change because of my grief life. I continue to wonder how he absorbed this and how this will affect his life.

My sister probably conceived her daughter the month our brother died—December. (Why does it seem like everyone passes right around the holidays?) I remember, many months later, when I was pregnant and sifting through his belongings after his death. Again, my parents were devastated (leveled). I thank God every day for my daughter and niece. I had been trying to conceive for over two years, and the idea that this could happen while I was stricken—floored after the death of Scott and then my brother—seemed impossible.

And I was desperate for another child. It had been twelve years since the birth of my first child. And I didn't want my son to be alone, God forbid. After all the death in my life, I was anxious about my own longevity. I needed to secure a sibling for my son.

I have so much empathy for those who want children but can't conceive. And there is much to be said about adoption and foster care. And I admire those who make a conscious choice not to have children. It's a culture on its own, fraught with prejudices. All I know is that for us, I feel utterly blessed that now my son has a sister and my parents, two more grandchildren.

I had finally secured a sibling for my son.

Bittersweet Babies

Bittersweet (adj.): pleasant but including or marked by elements of suffering or regret

I think the quietest form of grief in our culture is in the miscarriage arena. We women are warned against announcing our pregnancies too early in case something happens. "Wait at least twelve weeks. Get through the first trimester."

Why? So we don't have to grieve? Just who and what are we attempting to avoid or spare? Is it so others won't know we are grieving? It's difficult for these women. I know from many personal and professional experiences that miscarriages are hard, sad, and unacknowledged in this way.

When I hear someone's story or family history and there is a gap in the sibling sequence, I ask, "Miscarriages?"

I often hear, "I don't know. I suppose there could have been."

Nobody talks about it.

I've had family members, friends, and clients who've had to endure the unimaginable delivery of their deceased baby. The term miscarriage doesn't do these moms justice. I know in some cases, these are called stillborns; again, I don't like it—not strong or horrific enough. And I've heard doctors callously make remarks about getting pregnant again, like buying a puppy after you've lost your dog.

When I was forty-five, I discovered I was pregnant. I felt horrified, shocked, panicked, *ill*! I was incapacitated. I had been on medications that made me worry about continuing the pregnancy—let alone my age! I immediately started making phone calls, trying to figure out my options. Within days, I decided to chill out and see what would happen. Luckily, I found my wonderful ob-gyn, who made it possible for me to chill—believe me, this was a struggle.

By the time I began to truly shed my worries and believe it would all be okay, I was days away from a scheduled amniocentesis. And after my daughter's amnio, I swore I'd never go through the waiting agony of *that* test again! I was finally excited at the prospect of another baby. My anxieties were alleviated, and we were making plans, preparing for the blessing. Would it be a boy or a girl? We were excited—thrilled.

And in an instant, it all changed.

The morning before my amnio, I went to the doctor's for a routine prep appointment, and I found out the fetus no longer had a heartbeat. It was devastating, and yet it was easy to go to the "it was meant to be" place. And we held our heads up high, as though it was all okay. No big deal. In the end, this was not too difficult as hardly anyone knew we were pregnant. However, I think this was around the time my need to move into our new house went into overdrive.

Jackie Oh-So-Stoic

*Stoic: (n.) one apparently or professedly indifferent to pleasure or pain;
unmoved by joy or grief, and submissive to natural law*

My paternal grandmother and her sister married cousins—a typical story for the times. Scottish Canadian transplants, they lived in a duplex in Boston. They each had a baby around the same time—my father and the cousin who died. I've been told they didn't talk about the child's death. I'm sure it was too sad, too hard. Yet I wondered about it. How awful it must have been for all of them. Did my toddler dad grieve the loss of his playmate? How did this affect him?

We women are raised to be stoic. This is one of my soap-box lecturettes on our culture's need to reward people for hiding their feelings. I use Jacqueline Kennedy Onassis as my example of how stuffing feelings turns into disease, and boy, did we reinforce her ability to stuff her feelings. I hadn't been born yet when JFK died, but that image of Jacqueline Kennedy at the funeral, and everyone stating proudly that she was remarkably stoic, is ingrained in my psyche. This great lady died from cancer at all-too-young an age. She also suffered a miscarriage and the death of an infant in the face of a public life.

I remember a case for which I had written "stoicness" in my notes. At the following session, however, I was perplexed, wondering why I had written this. The client had wept throughout the entire session. When I think of stoicness, I think of flatness. Like being leveled. This client had been leveled. She had experienced the excruciating death of a child, an eighteen-month-old son. Curiously, it came to me as "stoicness"—the correct word actually is *stoicism*. (I often feel the need to add the "ness.") The tears were leaking out of this woman's eyes, yet her responses were matter-of-fact—a matter of flat. She, too, was a part of the cultural phenomenon that believed there must be something wrong with her because she was suffering. And so the stoicism continues.

I was surprised to learn that JFK and my grandmother were born in the same year. It gives a placement for the times, an idea about the why—the stoicism. These photos of those who died, before their time, lock us in time. It helps me understand my grandmother, my father, and perhaps my mom. When JFK died, my mom was about to give birth to me, her third child. She was in the worst month of pregnancy, the one where you just want the thing out of you. Where you can't wait any longer. I can't imagine what that time was like for her, amid all of the other issues going on at the time. Here she was, being the "perfect" housewife, who was slowly dying inside. She left her biology major at Smith College in her senior year to be with her first love at the University of South Carolina. She then became a wife and mother—not that there's anything wrong with that, though I'm certain this created much conflict in her family. And contributed to her depression.

When I was in high school, I saw many of these types of moms—the ones who disappeared, emotionally, and physically, mentally and spiritually. It reminds me of a John Singer Sargent portrait. His paintings are oil, handsome, and pleasing to the eye. You literally see the surface, the canvas. You don't necessarily see the physical pain of the subject of the painting—woman who has been sitting on that chair, for example, in that position, for hours and hours and hours. The artist has shown us what he (or the model) wants us to see. In Sargent's case, for me, it was a beautiful portrait of a beautiful woman. The stoicism, not the hardship. Or possible depression.

When I worked as an editor for a book company and wholesaler, I came across many interesting books. This was Berkeley and a cooperative company, very progressive, that had a small-press niche. It was at this company that I learned of the historical tradition of photographing the dead. We sold beautiful books on this subject matter, artistic. Before this job, I hadn't known this part of our history or that this was a part of our grieving many years ago. I studied these photos. I pondered this practice. This was at a time when nobody smiled in photos. They appear stoic. I think about it often today—how and when the process of photographing the dead changed (again, this is not a research book), but I wonder about the calendar of it all—the years, decades, and centuries. It intrigues me.

The Calendar Calamity

Calamity (n.): an extraordinarily grave event marked by great loss and lasting distress and affliction

The calendar of grief. It can be interesting, but who wants to examine it? I remember discussing this with my great pastor friend (whose father had passed rather suddenly —a great humanitarian and bishop in the Methodist Church). We wondered about the statistics on months and dates and deaths. I'm sure there is much to this. Just as there are certain months which produce a greater number of births, is this also true for deaths?

I said to my friend, "Sure, let's interview a bunch of people about when their loved ones died—not how, what, where, or why. Just the when."

We didn't think that would go over too well--asking people about the deaths of their loved ones in terms of dates. We tried not to giggle, but that's how we are. We find comfort in the humor, yet it doesn't negate our debates. We thought seriously about examining it as the two of us would—philosophically and spiritually.

Recently, a friend's mom died right before Christmas. Maybe we all have experiences of loved ones passing in December or in the beginning of January. My nonpastor other friend and I ended up having a conversation about why so many seem to transition at this time of year. Though it may seem like cruel irony, I told her, I wonder about the month being so holy, energetically, for all faiths. Many people attend church or temple, often one of the two times of the year they attend. There are lights, candles, and decorations everywhere. Prayers, hymns, dancing. People think and act generously—for the most part (some people are stress monsters). Still, is there a stronger magnetic pull at this time, as opposed to February, when much of the United States seems like dead and dread? Or spring, when life is giving birth to itself in all ways?

Days before Christmas, I told my friend who was grieving the loss of her mom, "Maybe it could be a comfort to your dad, knowing she was welcomed by more angels than at any other time of the year."

I wasn't sure what I believed. I believe in the possibility of just about anything. I believe we are greeted with intense love when we transition into our next realm. This is a bewildering comfort for many, yet perhaps not a comfort at all for many others.

The calendar is all about life and death, rebirth and renewal. We all have our personal love/hate relationships with certain dates and months. When I was younger, I would have said I loved autumn. It was my favorite time of year. Growing up in Michigan, cider mills abound. The smells are intoxicating. Now, I don't care for the month of October; it is connected to loss. I don't welcome what's coming. And I don't like the fact that it is suddenly dark outside when it should be light. I look out the window, and it is a surprise. And with PTSD, I startle easily, though I'm more conscious now of why this is so. Nevertheless, being jumpy is like having mini-heart attacks regularly. It's a rush I'd gladly shed if I could.

I'm also opposed to the time-change. My mind and my body have an objection to it. This contributes to the spookiness I feel in the air around Halloween. *Dias de los Muertos*, which takes place around the same time as Halloween, was one of Scott's favorite holidays, which I have tried to honor and appreciate, now that he has passed. I am very grateful he influenced my altar practice.

Ultimately, Halloween brings up grief. All Hallow's Eve commemorates the passing of souls. I think I must be plugged into this somehow, or maybe it was all those Halloween movies with which I terrorized myself—another aspect of the adrenaline junkie—at a young age. I do find this time of year unsettling. Maybe because I know what's around the corner, the stress holidays invite.

This time of year is tough for the grieving. On one hand, it is harvest time—beautiful colors, pumpkin patches, grape-stomping, children gleeful with anticipation. And on the other hand, winter is pending—and those often-dreaded holidays. I see the stress with many of my clients. The early darkness each day can trigger depression; the coming winter threatens and fosters it as well. I tend to turn on more lights at this time, warding off any chance of the uninvited.

The calendar is a constant reminder for the grieving, and holidays are its highlights. In the early years following the death of my mom, May was a month I dreaded, and two of my sisters would go into a depression of sorts. My mother died on Mother's Day; her birthday was a week later. For years, May packed a triple-whammy: birth, death, and Mother's Day. After my son's birth, all of this evaporated, and I celebrated being a mom in a big way—a fancy brunch or breakfast in bed. It feels extravagant, and it matters to me—a special time with my children.

For me, holidays and birthdays and death days were all a drag. I just wanted to forget all of them. Sometimes I did. And sometimes still do.

The calendar of grief.

Lousy Liberation

Liberation (n.): The act or process of trying to achieve equal rights and status

As I think about the grief calendar, I remember the month of July. My brother was born just after the fourth. This was an added celebratory event, as celebrating the Fourth of July is one of my parents' major traditions. We combined celebrations—my father's and sister's birthdays also are in this jumble. July has become been a mixed bag for me now. Do we celebrate my brother's life? Is it too hard for my dad? How do we celebrate everyone's birthday with this sad death in the mix? And then there is Independence Day—freedom.

Liberation—I'm thinking about the liberation (and grief) you experience when you lose your parents in the expected way (from old age). It's a silent, secret freedom from their judgment—for lack of a better word. Not that all parents are judgmental or that all adult children constantly or consciously care what their parents think, but this dynamic is inherent in the nature of the parent/child relationship. And it doesn't diminish the profound emptiness and loss we experience when our parents die.

In many respects, liberation is one of those tricky grief experiences. For instance, there's the relief one feels after watching a loved one linger, suffer, and fade away; where the loved one is no longer himself. We must feel a little freed by this situation, yet how can we allow ourselves to go there?

I remember this situation after my paternal grandfather died. My Grampy. When he died, my Grammy became a "nude" woman. I love to say nude instead of new, because it was as if she was reborn. She was freed. Now, Grampy didn't die after a long-suffering illness, but he had been terribly depressed after breaking his hip and feeling useless. He was the man who was always tinkering, forever working on something. He could build a house from the ground up—and did, many times. And Grammy had been his partner for over sixty years, so the few years he lived after he broke his hip were challenging. After he died, naturally she missed him very, very much. She talked to him all of the time. She told me she still slept on the same side of the bed. She couldn't free herself to hog the bed, but she had a lift in her step not long after he died.

For my friends and clients who are caregivers, I can say the unspeakable: "It's as though it might have been easier if the loved one died suddenly in a car accident … if he [or she] had to leave us anyway."

This is validating a feeling that cannot be expressed, but I can hold that truth for them. This is only in those unbearable terminal situations, where there is agonizing suffering, and it is an untenable and bleak circumstance.

And then there are those who have suffered tremendous loss and lose themselves in the aftermath, never moving forward. This can be a way of denying the loss ever happened. It seems to take over their entire identity. Perhaps the most excruciating are the ones who want to cling to the relationship, no matter what. They cannot turn off the life support, however that may look, no matter what misery is occurring. The anguish and agony line has become blurred. Is this about the dying or the loved one about to be left? And there will be no liberation.

Dogs and Divorce

And (conj.): used as a function word to express logical modification, consequence, antithesis, or supplementary explanation

Divorce is a form of liberation, yet it is also a death—of the marriage. This is a confusing and conflicting time for most, though there are cases of denial and some when it was clearly the right thing to do, such as when the marriage included safety issues or violence. When I got a divorce, it was my choice—I left the marriage. I'd been married for only three years, yet I grieved, to the degree I could (I know now that I'm not a good griever). I remember feeling lost and desperate. I recall wondering why I wasn't feeling free and happy. Liberated. After all, I was the one who wanted out. I immediately moved to a little island near my old home but soon after, I moved farther and farther away—so I didn't have to face it. (I'm sure this is true on some level, though I had valid reasons for my choices at the time.)

It is my contention that we don't honor the process of grieving where divorce is concerned. We believe we should be over it fairly quickly. We should move on. We encourage this. Others encourage us to start dating. I have encouraged this, sometimes. I've seen many, however, who chose to leave and are surprised by the transition, the difficulty of it all. I explain the grief piece and the stages, because we forget that there is a loss. After all, we are liberated. And then there are those times where we divorce because of a betrayal. This is a challenging change, and recovery will take quite some time, perhaps a lifetime, because betrayal is akin to the explosion of a bomb. If you leave a marriage with integrity (no betrayal), there will be hurt; if your marriage dissolves because of flagrant misbehavior (betrayal), there will be devastation. And a whole lot of damage. When you have to dig yourself out of the rubble, it hurts. And there will be scars, at least, and broken hearts at most.

Marriage is representative of so many things. For me, because it was brief, it was the loss of the "happy family" dream. I had a toddler son, and it was hugely his loss that I had to face every hour of every day. Divorce is so damaging for children, and we, as parents, need to address this and process it thoroughly. I think we've lost sight of this damage through statistics. People hear the nightmare stats—50 percent of marriages end in divorce—and somehow this diminishes the punch delivered by the breakup of the marriage—and perhaps diminishes the punch of the initial commitment. Have these statistics made people enter this promise with lighter resolve? Either way, the dissolution still hits us hard.

I think it's similar with pets, and how we honor these losses. Dogs, cats—our unconditional loves. We can have very soulful connections with our four-legged friends—I have. And yet we are pretty much forced to grieve in silence when these relationships end. We are ashamed to be so destroyed by the loss. We hear, "It's just a pet."

And yet the loss is devastating. I acquired my first dog when I was eighteen, a shepherd wolf named Bandit. He was an extraordinary animal and my best bud. I could write a whole book on our adventures. When he died, sixteen years later, I was so traumatized that my father and I *immediately* buried him, without thinking. My parents happened to be passing through from out of town for *one hour*—the hour he died. He wasn't ill, just old. I think Bandit planned it this way. My stepmother quickly whisked my son away to buy flowers for the gravesite. My father and I went into what I call PTSD mode. React. As we were placing my best four-legged friend on a blanket, I looked down and saw something I'd never seen before. I call it his death aura.

I said to my dad, "Wow, look at that—it looks like he has been sprinkled with baby powder."

My dad couldn't see it. I attribute this to my deep and soulful connection with my Bandit. My new missing contact.

I moved from that house soon after and have regretted leaving him there ever since, burying him so quickly without considering options. I didn't know about the whole pet cremation industry at the time, but I could have found out *if I had taken some time.* I kind of like the idea of having his ashes in a box marked Bandit—though it'd be one more thing to move. And we had places he loved, where we shared good times. I wish I had spread his ashes in the ocean at his favorite beach, Muir Beach—that would be so much easier to digest than the idea of his remains in someone else's yard.

Another agonizing animal event that may have kicked my most recent move into another gear was when one of our cats, Betty, was taken by a coyote. Betty was my husband's baby. She was a classic scaredy-cat—she would rarely go outside and was usually lying on our bed. She was the black furry blob you could count on seeing peripherally. She was short, overweight, and had a paunch. And I would encourage her to go out to get some fresh air and exercise—in the backyard, where it was safe. And she was usually reluctant. She was happy indoors and out of harm's way. But she had been getting braver, venturing out and about. Ironically, Betty's braveness was the result of her relationship with our own pet coyote, who is so loving that Betty couldn't hide from her constant licks and love. And this gave her confidence.

My husband discovered her death when he returned home after being gone for two weeks. The night before, I'd noticed my other cat, Pink, was behaving strangely. His eyes were noticeably tragic, and I thought he must have suddenly been stricken with cancer. He was leveled.

Things had been hectic with my husband gone for two weeks and when he returned, he asked me where Betty was, "I don't know. She's around here somewhere," I replied.

She was always around somewhere. But not this time. She was gone.

After a thorough search, I put two and two together. Pink must have witnessed her demise. We had heard there was a pack of very large coyotes roaming the streets in the early hours of the morning. We had been somewhat warned. Pink is our Thomas O'Malley cat. The cool cat with the swagger. He is too smart and agile to be caught, but Betty was another story. She was younger, but her only challenge was jumping on and off the bed. It all made sense. In my busyness, I had neglected the welfare of my cat. And I felt tremendous guilt. I still find my mind drifting back to Betty. Two years later, I still feel bad that I was so distracted, that I didn't protect her. I threw her to the wolves. I spent two weeks searching for her carcass so I could bury her properly—or do something. As if.

That was it. Another blow. We were outta there.

My Residual Mallard Unhappiness

Residual (adv.): an internal aftereffect of experience or activity that influences later behavior

In my new practice, these grief cases showed up more often. Naturally, I knew how to help them. I'd been there. I got it. I no longer referred these cases out, but I needed to be careful of my own possible countertransference. Simply put, countertransference is the therapist's emotional reactions to the client. It is critical for therapists to be conscious of this, so we don't respond based on our own needs, rather than the needs of the client. This is a therapist's mantra: do no harm. Keep your own stuff in check. It's like having a red flashing light in the corner of my consciousness. Sometimes countertransference is impossible to manage without the insight of another therapist—for consultation. This is the responsible and professional action.

I was conscious of my own grief and my shared experiences, but I hadn't made the connection between these and my moves. If I saw a client who recently had suffered a loss and advised that person to move, this would be an example of my countertransference interfering with the therapy. It has potential for harm. Obviously, it is especially difficult when I am struggling with a present experience.

Another and fairly benign example: in this new town, my attracting grief cases made it necessary for me to arrive early and practice what I call my "angel meditation." Just a contemplative, simple, quiet time for centering. This practice is also protective. It makes me feel like I have a shell around me, a soft one that prevents me from being consumed by the energy that surrounds me. This doesn't always go well, and this one particular morning, I was "off"—a sick residual feeling from the previous night's events.

I was driving home with my family at dusk on a fairly busy street. In the middle of the road was a male mallard, standing next to his female companion, who had been hit by a car. It was distressing. We pulled over and decided to move the female off the road, so the mate wouldn't get hit. She had just died, as she was still warm. We placed her in some bushes, hidden from the homes and traffic, in a canyon. The male followed. We waited five or so minutes, wondering and distraught. We were all silent on the ride home—sorrowful. I was certain I wasn't the only one thinking about the coyotes that would soon arrive to this pitiful scene.

The next morning, fourteen hours later, as I was driving down the canyon road to work, I slowed down to see if there was anything to see. There was the devoted male, still holding vigil for his lost mate. I'm not sure which would have been worse—seeing him or not seeing him. I was deeply moved and felt quite sick at heart.

My office is my sanctuary, and I hope it is for my clients as well. I wanted to be sure I'd shaken this mallard unhappiness. I'd certainly worked under more trying personal experiences than this one, but for some reason, this situation moved me. It was touching and miraculous. What exactly had I witnessed? And how was I going to get it? I was searching for my lesson. And it was a potential distraction from my clients.

When my best friend was dying, when I found out it was imminent, I jumped in my car and madly drove down to the Bay Area, an hour away, without notice. My great friend and confidant called my clients and explained the situation. And again, when my brother died. This was obviously delicate (confidentiality—protecting my clients privacy) as I could only give her first names, very specific dialogue, and, for me, this was unprecedented. I was flying by the seat of my pants.

When I returned to work, over a week later, my clients were curious and concerned. And I told them of my loss. Both times. Otherwise, it would have been sitting there in the middle of the room, blocking our view of each other, our capacity for connection. Of course, we had to process the possibilities this could produce in terms of caretaking issues for them and myself, but my one statement—"It's honestly easier for me to focus on you than it ever has been"—was remarkably true. And they understood. Working while grieving was eerily easy. It's the other stuff that can get in the way.

Oh My, Meds

My (adj.): used interjectionally with names of various parts of the body to express doubt or disapproval

E very now and then, I have clients with whom I very delicately bring up the topic of medication—antidepressants. For reasons obvious to me, their depression or anxiety is significantly affecting their level of functioning. Many, many years ago, I performed stand–up comedy and had an entire routine based on Prozac and a *Stepford* theme. And it was completely ignorant (but got laughs). As a practitioner, I see the benefits of psychotropic medications. It has helped many of my people (family, friends, and clients). I explain that I understand the whole weakness idea and how, at one time, I unconsciously endorsed this idea that we should be able to handle anything.

When I was in my early thirties, single parenting, running around across county lines, trying to be the best parent, therapist, and human I could be, I got mono for the third time—a medical mystery. I was knocked down. I couldn't commute to my job, my "piles" (things that needed attending) were growing, and I was drowning. I went to see my nurse practitioner, whom I trusted, to get her sign-off for disability. She suggested I go on Prozac.

I was aghast.

"I'm not *depressed*; I have *mono!*" I exclaimed, through floods of tears and shakes.

"It will help," she said as she handed me six weeks' worth of samples.

I decided to take the medication and it helped. The piles still grew, but they seemed manageable, and I stopped being so overly concerned about them.

It was a great lesson for me and one I've shared many times.

I tell my people, "You can call the doctor and make the appointment. You can show up. You can get a prescription, if the doctor or nurse practitioner agrees. You can fill the prescription. You can pick it up. You can put it in your medicine cabinet. You can take it, if you want to. But if you don't make the initial call, you don't have the options."

I also warn them, "If you take this medication, you need to follow the directions. You cannot start it and stop it. You can't stop taking it because you feel better. You need to titrate off it, and treat it seriously. Talk to your doctor about this. And I do believe there is immediate symptom relief, though the six-week plan is about the side effects and effectiveness. It takes a while for the chemistry to adjust. Remember, this is not a happy pill. But I believe it will help. And if at any time we need to evaluate this, we will, with your doctor—just don't do it on your own!"

Again, I only recommend this when I see a client in need, someone whose weepiness or anxiety is truly interfering with his or her life. And I share my own experience, because I know the resistance and want to take the shame and stigma away. This resistance is powerful. We believe we should be able to manage our lives, even in the face of all the evidence (I was drowning). It is so hard to watch people struggle with debilitating anxieties or depression, knowing there is help out there, but they flat out refuse to accept medication. They could be living a different life, a life free from incapacitating fear. Mind you, I take this very seriously. There are many valid alternatives to psychotropic medicine but sometimes, it is warranted, and it helps. If we could just get past the shame.

PART 2

OH SH**T! SHAME!

.

It's Okay to Be A-C-o-A

Well, I searched and Googled and researched, and the only thing I could come up with as a definition of ACoA was the one I already knew—Janet G. Woititz's characteristics, developed in 1983. I actually thought there would be a definition from the American Psychiatric Association. I guess this is a good thing. (Why am I looking to pathologize myself?) I have a chapter of Woititz's book photocopied and hand it out often to clients who grew up with any dysfunction—not necessarily alcoholism; anything that has left them with residual feelings of shame or abandonment. When I got together with my husband, and it seemed necessary, I gave him a copy. Even though I had done my work, I wanted him to understand where I came from. Here are the characteristics of adult children of alcoholics:

1) *ACoAs guess at what normal is.*

2) *ACoAs have difficulty in following a project through from beginning to end.*

3) *ACoAs lie when it would be just as easy to tell the truth.*

4) *ACoAs judge themselves without mercy.*

5) *ACoAs have difficulty having fun.*

6) *ACoAs take themselves very seriously.*

7) *ACoAs have difficulty with intimate relationships.*

8) *ACoAs overreact to changes over which they have no control.*

9) *ACoAs constantly seek approval and affirmation.*

10) *ACoAs feel that they are different from other people.*

11) *ACoAs are either super-responsible or super-irresponsible.*

12) *ACoAs are extremely loyal, even in the face of evidence that loyalty is undeserved.*

13) *ACoAs tend to lock themselves into a course of action without giving serious consideration to alternative behaviors or possible consequences. This impulsivity leads to confusion, self-loathing, and loss of control of their environment. As a result, they spend tremendous amounts of time cleaning up the mess.*[9]

You may recognize this material. I believe and have seen some of these characteristics apply to persons who maybe didn't have an alcoholic parent but an unavailable one, for whatever reason. We all have a little bit of everything in us. It's when it is out of balance that things go awry, and we may have a disorder.

As with many disorders, these labels can be offensive to people. We reject them—ADHD, PTSD, ACoA—outright in the face of all evidence; understandably so, I guess. After all, any piece of these descriptions can send us reeling with anxiety and fear. It's only a piece. As I teach in my compulsive-eating groups, a piece of anything is perfectly all right. Just don't swallow the whole pie.

This is especially true with personality disorders. These "labels" are tossed around regularly.

Such as, "He's a narcissist."

Yet these are serious conditions.

As a psychotherapist, I occasionally have to provide a diagnosis for insurance purposes. I use the DSM-IV—this is my diagnostic bible (Diagnostic and Statistical Manual.) Occasionally, I hold it up for clients and explain that it has nearly one thousand pages of disorders, divided into various sections. In my graduate program, there was a one-semester class to learn the material. The personality disorder (PD) section, however, is only about thirty-five pages, yet it takes another semester to begin to understand it.

Personality disorders are complex. They are developed in the very earliest stages of life, when trust is created. The infant can only see approximately ten inches—the distance between the nipple (or bottle) and the mother's eyes—thereby gaining reassurance from the mom, dad, or primary caregiver that the world is a safe place and all is well. It develops trust.

For many reasons, some obvious and others much less so, this trust doesn't always develop. And this is a finite version of a very complicated crystal. Also, there are many complicated cases that beat the odds—don't end up with this diagnosis. While others seem to come out of nowhere—though I think there is a root source if explored. It is my belief (although I'm sure many experts would have different opinions) that personality disorders are more rare than we think, and those labeled as narcissists are more likely to have traits rather than the full-blown disorder. Maybe I just want to believe this.

Personally, I find the labels or diagnoses to be helpful, and mostly, my clients do as well, with gentle guidance and understanding. After all, we wouldn't have these labels if there weren't many of us coping with these conditions or circumstances. It was a great relief to me when I read Woititz's books, and I learned much about myself and my being an ACoA. It also meant I wasn't alone. And my patterns, my feelings, and my behaviors were a natural result of my upbringing.

I call it our makeup. But in the end, that's all it is. Makeup. Something we use to see ourselves in a different light. And makeup can come in handy. I use this definition in a broad way, which includes hair product, clothes, perfume—anything that makes us feel better or changed. Our true self, our true light, is underneath the makeup, the labels, the physical. It cannot be seen. And it's much more powerful than any piece of makeup. It's the divine, which has no face yet is working through us, wanting our highest good. And the good news, make-up is an application easily removed.

It's Psychotherapy, Not Psychobabble

Psychobabble: (a portmanteau of "psychology" or "psychoanalysis" and "babble") is a form of prose using jargon, buzzwords, and highly esoteric language to give an impression of plausibility through mystification, misdirection, and obfuscation (from Wikipedia)[10]

We humans reject the possibility of a diagnosis outright because of fear, shame, and judgment. I'm terribly afraid of being judged by writing this book. And there will be those who will judge me. I have to keep my eye on the ball—the "I want to help people" ball. A medicine ball of sorts.

The idea of seeing a therapist can have the same response. We avoid therapy for these very reasons—fear, judgment—and because we *know*, perhaps unconsciously, that it may be tremendously difficult, uncomfortable—and painful. So we make excuses. We call it malarkey. It takes courage to enter therapy, and courage is stepping into the fire, even though there is fear. It is bravery.

People often ask me about being a therapist. My usual spiel is that there is the misconception that someone must be crazy (mentally ill—most don't even know what this is) to see a therapist. The truth is that "crazy" people don't voluntarily enter into therapy. Most people who enter my therapy office are intelligent, open-minded, thoughtful people who want to transform their lives. They recognize there is something, big or little, blocking this process, and they are smart enough to know it is helpful to have an outside observer guide them. And I feel blessed to have work I love to do.

Many people come in thinking there will be a quick fix. They come in with a time limit in mind: six weeks, three months, one year. Although I know that true transformation, if you really want to change the circumstances of your life, takes much longer than one year, I rarely divulge this to my clients. It would just scare them off. Yes, it takes time. When I recognize a person's capacity for the work, a person who truly wants to change an old behavior that he or she recognizes as a roadblock, I am sometimes upfront about the length of time it may take. I ask for a commitment—but very rarely in the first session.

Therapy can be exhausting. The time of day and day of the week you see your therapist is a practical concern, because it is trying. I have noticed clients who see me on their lunch hour are much less likely to break down, as they know they'll be back at the office in one hour. In these cases, when necessary, I try to see them at the end of the day. The scheduled time isn't helping the process; in fact, it's stagnating. There is a little strategy involved in the psychotherapeutic process. For instance, optimally, I try to schedule clients at the same time each week. It helps with the process. When a person comes in twice a week, it's even more beneficial. Not only is this most advantageous because it's twice as often, but the relationship deepens faster and the work as such. When someone wants to come in every other week, I explain that my experience is that this type of gap in the process can make it seem as if we are starting over at each session, rather than deepening where we are.

When I am working with a serious eating disorder, my protocol is two sessions a week, a meeting with a nutritionist once a week, and monthly blood work. You can see how this could be overwhelming (and scare people off). Yet I insist. And I lose many clients because of this. And sometimes, they come back later, when the damage is more ingrained, and the work is twice as challenging. My protocol is particularly important with eating disorders because I often meet the client *before* the disorder is entrenched. And afterward, when the client comes back, it is most often entrenched and there can be a lifelong and dangerous battle with something that should provide pleasure—food, a very basic necessity and wonderful part of our lives.

And then there are the couples, who *really* do not want to be in my office. Often, one of them has been dragged in against his or her will. I have to be very careful not to alienate one-half of the couple. It's a balancing act sometimes. And then, there are the times when I say something that strikes a chord—and they don't come back. The woman is angry, offended; the man feels validated. Or vice versa.

I tell my couples, "Marriage is like a car. You have to maintain it, or there will be problems. Eventually, and maybe more than once, you will need to see the mechanic. I am your mechanic, and I don't anticipate my office closing. You can always come back when you recognize a weird noise that needs attention. Or for a tune-up."

And most satisfying are my clients who go away to college—satisfying, because most often they've graduated from the therapy. I think of them after they've "graduated" and wonder how old they are now and what they're doing. For me as a therapist, these are my most ambivalent departures. For many, I watched them individuate. I played a special part. Even though they leave me, they don't leave my thoughts.

What about the cost? I sometimes think of it as a luxury. And luxuries are pricey but worth it. Two and a half years of weekly therapy, where real transformation occurs, generally adds up to less than ten thousand dollars. Sounds like a lot of money until you put it in perspective. You are investing in *your life* or *your child's life*. Isn't it worth it? Aren't *we* worth it? We invest in our vehicles, our jewelry, our art, our homes, and our toys. Why not in ourselves? Inpatient treatments are costly, even if insurance is involved, yet we want the quick fix, the one that will never work (in extreme cases of eating disorders or addiction) without follow-up therapy. (The average stay at an inpatient clinic is 28 days—dictated by insurance.)

I asked my husband why he thinks people are so afraid of therapy. He can be dead on when it comes to first instincts about others. I trust his judgment completely.

He said, "People don't want to deal with their issues."

Really? Even though these issues are swallowing them up? Experience says yes, really. Remember, I avoided therapy myself when I probably needed it most.

We would do anything to save our children, yet we are incapacitated by the idea of therapy. Is this about secrecy? Shame? What will be discovered? It can't be worse than what is already happening. And we would do anything for our health if we received a dreaded diagnosis, such as cancer. We would mortgage our homes, sell off our toys, to save our health. Yet when it comes to our psychological and spiritual health, we lose perspective. I guess that's because of the shame, stigma, and our false beliefs.

I also believe true transformation occurs when we have a solid spiritual practice. You can do and have a spiritual practice anywhere—on a mountain, in your bedroom, or in your backyard. I encourage people to create a special place for meditation and make it nice. Make it a place for stillness.

Have You No Shame?!

Shame (n.): a condition of humiliating disgrace or disrepute

I believe and teach that guilt is a normal human emotion. It is part of being a conscious and caring person. Shame, however, is a toxic form of guilt, just as rage is the toxic form of anger. Guilt might not feel good but it is a natural emotion; shame doesn't feel good at all and is, in fact, hurtful. Maybe guilt takes up too much space in our brain, but in the end, it's not such a bad thing. Sometimes, it's even helpful, as an opportunity for growth.

When shame appears, we feel sick. We can't stop thinking. We can't stop doing. We can't stop. And it binds us up like a mummy. I believe shame is behind most addictions. It's a vicious cycle, because it results in behaviors that leave us feeling even more shamed. Shame also causes unhealthy rumination. It is intolerable. It keeps us from sleep. It keeps us from living fully and most important, from being our authentic self. There is no shame in nature. We are not meant to have shame or be shameful. This is an outpicturing of our human experience, our circumstances, which has nothing to do with our true self. Yet there it is. Usually, every day in my office. Sometimes, there are days in my own life. The old "shoulda, woulda, coulda," the critic.

This shame was most likely inflicted on us by our parents (or primary caregiver), the one that forgot to tell us we are good, beautiful, intelligent, light, love, life, wisdom, peace … all the qualities of the god (our true selves) talked about in all religions. These are the qualities in all things, if you look. If we open our eyes, beyond what is feeding us from the human source, this is all you see. There is nothing else. I love the artists who take garbage and make beautiful and stimulating pieces for our pleasure. They see the potential when it is raw.

Shame is a human manifestation, yet it is so difficult to break down. It begins when we are young. I recall my first shameful memory while in my first-grade class. It involved my knowing for sure that I had the right answer to my teacher's question. I waved my arm up as high as I could. The teacher called on me. And my answer was wrong. I distinctly recall the flush of shame I felt at being so full of myself.

When we think about the children we know, naturally, the world revolves around them. It is supposed to do so. We are meant to celebrate *their* universe; it is most precious and enriching. For me, any experience or conversation with children is rewarding and healing, whether it's cooing to an infant or struggling with an angry adolescent. I love them all.

Heinz Kohut, a psychoanalytic psychotherapist, developed the theory that resonated with me the most in graduate school. His theory of self-psychology purports that children need to develop three things for a healthy, whole self. First, they need to develop the grandiose self. This happens when a parent rewards the child with praise. For instance, Joey says, "Dad, watch me throw this ball!" And Dad watches and responds, "Great, Joey. You are so good at that!" Children need constant mirroring and validation.

Second, the child needs to develop the idealized self. This occurs when the child knows the parent is greater than any frightening circumstance. For instance, after a thunderclap, the child feels frightened and runs to his parents. Mom and Dad reassure the child that they will protect him, and it'll be okay. And the child is soothed.

Third, the child needs to develop the twinship self, which encompasses his or her need to be like others. The child goes to school and feels like the other kids. He has a sense of belonging. You may see how easily the development of one or more of these selves can be thwarted. In any situation where a parent is not emotionally or physically available—parents who have issues with drinking, working to excess, travel, mental illness, narcissism—the child is unable to develop a cohesive self; a healthy, whole self. This is where therapy comes in. The therapist can provide the mirroring, the idealizing, and the twinship that was missing. And it works!

When we grow up without these parents or primary caregivers , the ones who nurture these parts of our selves, we often struggle with issues of shame and guilt. When I feel shame, it is as if my whole body goes toxic at once. The only way I can explain it is like this: when we blush, we get that flushed feeling in our cheeks. When I feel shame, the flush starts in my toes and rapidly moves up to my head, enveloping every cell and tissue in between. And then it takes refuge in my mind, where it can ruminate and grow. I don't have these experiences often anymore, thank goodness, and I'm grateful that I know it when it's happening. Because when it does, I literally can't sleep—that's when it most often occurs for me. I wake up in the middle of the night, the flush has occurred, and the mental part is in full flurry.

When I was in my early twenties—oh, the things that used to keep me up. The "Why did I say that?" Or the "I hope she [or he] didn't think ..." Typical codependent shame and rumination. Now, I have great tools to combat any negative thoughts, beginning with my mind. I can choose new thoughts. Good thoughts; reminders that I'm a good person, a good daughter, wife, and mom. (I'm remembering *Saturday Night Live*'s funny sketch with Al Franken in the '80s, where his character looks in a mirror and tells himself, "Because I'm good enough ..." Funny but true. These tools work.)

However, there was a time when my shame was attached to truly shameful behaviors. Remember, as an ACoA, any behavior that feels "overboard" has the potential to leave me wracked with shame.

Argh, the Abandonment

Abandonment (n.): complete disinterest in the fate of what is given up, desolation

Every time this word *abandonment* is uttered from my chords, I cringe a bit, even though I own my own abandonment issues. I feel a shuddering, some kind of fear, like horror. It's as if hearing a therapist say, "It sounds like you may have an abandonment issue," is a death sentence, to be whispered only. Shameful. This word has so many implications, false meanings, and important insights. I love the dictionary definition because it takes me to the literal meaning, yet it encompasses the psychological so well.

In psychology, having an abandonment issue implies we had an emotionally and/or physically unavailable parent. For whatever reason, our primary caregiver "abandoned" us. And because of this, not only might we have issues, but bad things could have happened that compounded our already developing abandonment issues. For instance, maybe our parent was single, working three jobs, and left us with the neighbors, and someone in that household molested us. I don't know anyone, however, who hasn't suffered some abandonment in his or her life, so why does it feel like a word that needs whispering? (Very extreme cases do create disturbing—whisper-worthy—circumstances and personalities.)

My own abandonment issues came from my mom being an alcoholic. She was a homemaker. And she took this seriously, did her best. She was the supermom, driving us to and from our many sports and lessons. From the outside, she was the typical, good, corporate businessman's wife. But she seemed to be daydreaming most of the time. Disassociating. And then, towards the end of this nuclear family, there were times when she drove on the wrong side of the road.

Though I know I was mirrored (validated) by my parents and have clear memories of this, I can assume the idealized aspects of myself could have been in question as a developing child. I know I felt a tenacious connection to the earth and its bounty; the universe and its possibilities; and the great unknown, God. This probably provided some aspect of the idealized self. A good one. When the thunder clapped, for me, it was Mother Nature waking us up. This made me feel less frightened. I know I felt completely different from all of my classmates. This twinship part, no doubt, was a missing piece, swallowed up by my abandoning mother experience, though I don't underestimate the power of our early adult experiences in reshaping our futures.

My stepmother came into my life two years before my mom died. She and my father, after various typical blended-family struggles, undoubtedly provided some missing pieces to my fragmented picture. We therapist types used to believe that our "selves" were determined in those first years of life. We now know that much more development occurs in adolescence and young adulthood. Thank goodness.

My saving grace was that I was cute and smart, and my teachers and coaches took an interest in me. I had many extraneous adults in my life who could supply me with a sense of safety. I think this is why I began my practice with adolescents. I could be one of the adults in their lives who could be there for them in this way.

And I could share my unyielding belief there was something greater looking out for me. Just as it was for them.

Angst and Anger

Anger (n.): emotional excitement induced by intense displeasure

I believe we are not comfortable with anger in our culture. It's almost taboo. We shut it down. And we like to hurdle right over it. And react. React, react, react. Maybe if we took the time, we could take the power and fear out of the feeling of anger. No more hiding, soothing, sweeping, hurdling ... or bombing. Let me be clear here: anger is healthy. Rage, which encompasses bitterness and maltreatment, is the toxic form of anger. Rage injures and is abusive. Anger provides the possibility for dialogue and change. Change is good. Change is constant.

A person's barometer reading for anger becomes part of an assessment in therapy, and very important with couples. Our comfort or discomfort level with anger is quite revealing. With couples, I ask each person— separately-- how his or her parent expressed anger. In my family of origin, my mom drank her anger. I'm not so sure about my dad. He drank, but mostly he worked a lot when I was young. Yet there was this thing he did with his teeth, where his lower teeth would jut out a little when he spoke, and we knew he was M-A-D!

Asking about their parents' anger is one of the most informative and helpful sessions for my clients. The idea is that we learn how to express anger from early experiences with our parents.

How many of us would say, "I never saw my parent's argue"?

And the issues this produced, like conflict avoidance.

The alternative might be, "I hid under the table while things flew across the room."

And all the things in between.

Many couples tell me they have never argued. This is a problem. You put different biology and personality in any room for a given period of time, and there will be issues. It's normal and natural. Yet, we are so afraid of it. What's important is to understand how we adapted these styles or chose the opposite style, purposefully, to the one we saw in our parents. There are repercussions, nonetheless.

In my own early therapy work, I didn't see the point of thinking about, feeling, or talking about anger. This was around the time I entered graduate school. My mom was dead. She was the one I was angry with.

I remember telling my therapist at the time, "Anger isn't necessary, and if I have any, it is probably in my pinky toe, very far from my heart, gut, mouth, and mind."

Virginia Woolf said, "The history of most women is hidden either by silence, or by flourishes and ornaments that amount to silence."

My loss of anger was my silence.

My silent grief.

And I know I learned this from my mom. She was very passive.

I now know that all relationships, living or dead, reflect back our work and what's in our hearts, minds, and guts. (At one point, my first husband actually started to look like my mom—that was when I entered therapy.) But my anger was a hidden compartment, the one behind the one you saw. The one you did see was the helper, the giver, the listener—the one who felt much but showed only glimpses. The one who ruminated later, much later, after the fact, and again, mostly at night. The one who said, "I can't believe she (could be anyone) did that."

And then, the instant forgiveness: "It must be about me."

And then, the "I can't believe *I* said that."

And the shadow part. The shadow is the bag we carry around which contains aspects of ourselves we'd like to discard—hence the invisible baggage. The shadow side for the caregiver—resentment and anger. It's the one that makes you feel like a doormat, while welcoming the repressed anger.

That Dreaded Word Codependence

Codependence (n.): A codependent is loosely defined as someone who exhibits too much, and often inappropriate, caring for persons who depend on him or her. A codependent is one side of a relationship between mutually needy people. The dependent, or obviously needy party, may have emotional, physical, or financial difficulties or addictions that he or she is seemingly unable to surmount. The codependent party exhibits behavior that controls, makes excuses for, pities, and takes other actions to perpetuate the obviously needy party's condition, because of his or her desire to be needed and fear of doing anything that would change the relationship.[11]

I have found that most people have a negative reaction to the word *codependent*. And they often have an incorrect definition. I occasionally ask what they think it means. I explain, very simply, that codependence is putting others' needs ahead of your own. Codependents are, at worst, people who stay with a batterer or an addict because they feel that person "needs" them. At best, codependents are doctors, nurses, teachers, psychotherapists—those who have channeled their innate nature into a profession. Hopefully, after we work through our own issues, we will practice with healthy boundaries. When we have unhealthy boundaries, people take advantage of us. When we have healthy boundaries, we take care of ourselves.

I consider my best work to be with codependent women and teens. It was the work I did in my own therapy, many years back. I was the peacemaker in my family. The one who tried to negotiate the truce. The glue. And glue is manufactured to be invisible yet must hold things together. When things were ugly, though, I tried very hard to blend into the paneling on the walls around me, not to be noticed. I created an inner world, a fantasy.

I remember being on a family vacation in Kentucky at a grand old lodge. It was supposed to be a fabulous family trip. My little sister ended up in the emergency room on that trip after cracking her head open. I have a clear memory of being in the lodge with all of the other families for dinner and searching for the family I wanted to live with. Yet this only made me feel terrible, as you can imagine—the peacemaker, dreaming of and searching for the clearest and easiest exit route. I've heard many in my practice say something very similar, describing a memory when they were admiring and envying other families and wondering why. And feeling very guilty about it.

The book I thought I'd write, when I arrived in this new town and was awaiting licensing, was called *When I Take Care of Myself, I Feel Selfish.* (I apparently love to toy with titles.) This came to me easily. I had heard this statement repeatedly from women and girls in my office. And I remembered the feeling well. The irony was that these were not selfish women—just the opposite. These women were giving, generous, nurturing, and loving, among other things. For them, it was like having a low-grade fever for years; we can work with it. We can grocery shop, cook dinner, go to soccer practice, and put on a happy face, but we don't feel fully right. Something is slowly taking the wind out of our sails. And there is suffering. Many had depression, at least a mild form (called *dysthymia*). They felt as though they were swimming upstream in tepid waters. They had no idea why they were weepy or struggling. Everything was so right in their lives.

I remember one client, a giving and caring woman, who was struggling with a relationship with another woman. My client was a stay-at-home mom. The other woman was working mom who asked if my client would watch her child after school; she would pick her up at five. My client had no problem with this ... initially. But the woman kept pushing back the time—the working mom was picking her child up later and later. And it was disrupting my client's family schedule. She didn't know what to do. She couldn't fathom that it was okay to say, "I don't mind having your child here, but it's important you pick her up on time. I need to take care of my family and keep my schedule on time."

Something so seemingly clear and easy was difficult for her.

I explained to her, "You will be modeling healthy boundaries, and she is asking for them. She will benefit from these good boundaries. People respond to healthy boundaries in a good way. Our fear is that we will hurt them, but in fact, we are helping them, because this is an issue for all of us. We need examples around us, and it doesn't hurt. You'll be surprised—if you set a boundary once, it will get easier the next time, because the world doesn't fall apart. You will experience a different response from what you expect. You deserve to take care of your family, and she deserves to know she is pushing the limits."

My validating this for her was what she needed. The good news is that this woman was smart enough to know something was off, and she sought an outside observer—a therapist. I could affirm and help transform her beliefs about what she deserved. I told her, "You deserve to have power in your relationships—to say no; to say yes; to say all things honestly; to love yourself; and to put yourself first."

This is not a selfish act. It's an act of empowerment that produces positive results. I know this to be true, yet unless we practice this, we won't see the outcome. When we do, the results are clearly visible, and it makes it so easy to do it again.

Those Blasted Boundaries

Boundary (n.): something that indicates or fixes a limit or extent

Naturally, healthy boundaries are critical to proper psychotherapy. I believe most Americans don't realize what healthy boundaries are. We tend to repeat what we know, and the American culture encourages a complete lack of boundaries, as evidenced on talk shows and reality shows, which, I believe, all began here in this country. I have a "boundaries lecturette" that I explain to most of my clients, because it is a huge part of the work. I believe a class on boundaries should be taught in high school.

Though I didn't anticipate abandoning my Napa clients, when I moved away, I did just that. I think I did good termination work with them before I left, but in the end, I'm sure some felt deserted. Looking back, I abandoned myself as well. I sometimes wonder what kind of person leaves a thriving practice in a beautiful, safe place and starts all over in a "foreign" state, where the boundaries are unknown? Now, I can come up with valid and brave reasons to justify this move, but as you know, I now see all of my moves as a grief reaction.

So what about boundaries? Where do they fit in? I believe boundaries are critical to living a good life, and as a therapist, they are even more critical and even more challenging—although this can be said for accountants, doctors, lawyers, ministers … okay, so maybe it's true for all professions. Confidentiality and privacy—these are important matters.

In my previous small-town practice, boundaries, ironically, were fairly easy. "Ironically," because it *was* a small town. I couldn't go anywhere without running into clients. Yet my practice was busy. I didn't have openings, so things were cut-and-dried. There were, however, a few instances where friends or fellow professionals wanted me to see their child. Or spouse. This was tricky. Initially, I would put them off and make recommendations. But they were relentless. Eventually, this line was crossed.

There were the necessary pre-therapy discussions; for example, "Okay, so you know if I see your teen, and it is clear that this is not her problem but yours, we will have to deal with this." And the response was usually, "Of course." I would only cross this line with those people I believed were able to handle and process at this level—the level that pointed the finger in their direction.

I was hardly ever able to enjoy the lovely, touristy town that I lived in—because of the client issue. It would not be appropriate for my clients to see me wine-tasting (at least, I thought so at the time). I now see this as a shame issue, more ACoA baggage! And there was my authenticity piece. I dashed through the farmer's market because it was just too awkward to run into people. There is the recommended discussion with clients, telling them that when we see each other out of the room, "I won't acknowledge you unless you acknowledge me." It's part of informed consent, where the psychotherapist explains the process of therapy. And I was often concerned with my appearance, when I just wanted to be in sweats and pick up milk, yet I knew the cashier. It was just easier to stay home.

In the new Nevada practice, new practices emerged. For instance, most therapists stick to certain hours—9:00 to 3:00. In the beginning, I had no set hours. As this was wreaking havoc on my body, schedule, and consequently, my family, I created a schedule and tried to stick with it.

Then I made the mistake of moving my office landline to my cell phone, trying to save a little money. Well, all of my clients could see I have an iPhone, so the questions about e-mail starting coming. And the texts just showed up, especially with my teens. To me, this is not only a pain but has the potential for major problems—texts are easily lost in the shuffle. I shudder to think of a teen texting her therapist that she is feeling lost, hopeless—suicidal.

I would guess by the tenth session, I've had a talk about boundaries with every client. Boundaries are the trickiest, however, with family. The way I deliver my boundaries lecturette for my clients is to hold my arms out wide. I explain on one side (my right hand) is enmeshment. Then I take my hands and weave my fingers together. This is where there are no boundaries. Worst case scenario: sexual abuse. Less-than-worst-case scenario: you tell your sister something you believe is confidential, and it quickly spreads through the family like wildfire.

With my arms wide open again, I say that on the left side are rigid boundaries. This is when someone says, "My mom doesn't talk to her brother—hasn't for years—but nobody knows what happened. We don't talk about it."

You can see the diametrical difference: one, too much openness; the other, no openness. Even though that has worked for me as a good educational method, each time I administer it, it strikes me hard, whether my clients see it or not. Again and again, boundaries are hugely important. And neither enmeshed nor rigid has direct healthy communication. Therapists strive for the healthy middle. And although we acknowledge cultural differences, it is still the goal to be in the middle—where the head and heart are.

Count on Calculus

Count (v.): to have value or significance

One of the more difficult hurdles, as a therapist, is the client who comes in with the "I need the answer for my calculus problem" hurdle. I love my teens who embrace calculus. The very word makes me go cross-eyed, yet they—my teen clients and my son—love it because it makes sense. You take a very complex problem and reduce it to a simple, precise answer. But therapy doesn't work like that. And neither does grief and shame.

I call these clients my product-seekers. And they are challenging but not uncommon. For me, it's difficult, as I like to provide answers and help out. Unfortunately, psychotherapy is mostly about the process. Though I think I educate my clients more than the average psychotherapist, I still know how critical it is for them to come to their own conclusions. This is also dependent on the type of work being done. A long-term analysis client calls for very different responses than HMO referrals, which usually are brief. Each situation is unique, yet change is truly integrated and transformative when clients figure out *on their own* what the change should be.

In my own therapy, my deep work, I sought an object relations therapist purposefully. Simply put, object relations theory is a derivative of psychoanalytic theory, and Kohut's self-psychology is a derivative of object relations. And it (the therapeutic relationship) was frustrating. My therapist would tell me nothing of herself. She had good boundaries, and I hated that. And though I wanted answers, I wouldn't ask the questions. I was the good client and student. I was in graduate school at the time, and she knew this. She would wait. And wait. And wait. And I would not ask. For instance, I was dying to know if she had kids. After all, did she even understand what it was like for me? Yet I would not ask the question. I understood the process. But let's face it—mostly it was a further example of my codependence. I was taking care of my therapist, and she knew it. She knew if I could ask the question, I was healing.

The therapy ended because I moved, though less than an hour away, depending on traffic. My therapist wanted me to continue our work. I couldn't fathom driving any more than I already was. I truly was burned out from a long commute after one year. We flushed out the issues, and in the end, I left. I dissected this for quite some time and again years later, after reading *The Thief of Happiness* by Bonnie Friedman, in which a client (the author) drives great distances to continue working with her object relations therapist. Did my therapist abandon me by not supplying the answers? Did this abandonment trigger intolerable shame? Could I not count on my therapist? Did I experience a grief issue that instigated my move (I absolutely did—at this point I was swimming in grief issues), and was my commute argument valid? Could I not tolerate the work? Was my work complete? Is a cigar a cigar?

What I recall was a struggle in the end. She wanted one thing; I wanted another. It was feeling like we were fighting. Certainly conflict was something I couldn't abide and most definitely not with my therapist. I remember being mad at her. And believing this was a good thing. With my own clients who have codependent tendencies, when they can be mad at me or something to do with me or my office, we are on the road to recovery—as long as we process it!

To Do, To Do, To Do, To Do

Do (v.): treat or deal with in any way typically with the sense of preparation or with that of care of attention

I've seen many clients and others with the very challenging Midwestern farmers work-ethic belief system—it's all too familiar. It's the one that says you can't sit still; you must produce; you must *do*. I believe this is triggered by shame or, at minimum, derived from shame. When I see clients, I tend to drum up their "constitution" in my mind. It helps me work. In my own constitution, I was a card-carrying member of the Midwestern Farm Workers Union. Now, my dues are long past due. There was a time when I couldn't relax. When I watched television, I had to be dusting, ironing, or organizing something. Anything that would justify the fact that I was doing something mindless like watching TV. I would do something productive so I could allow myself do something purposeless. A little crazy.

This belief (being the busy, hard worker) can be damaging yet prolific. Either way, it is seductive to the grief-stricken. It is why many latent cases of obsessive-compulsive disorder begin with a trauma. The easiest way to avoid (and soothe) horrible pain or shame is to do, to do, to do, to do, to do. (I'm reminded of Glinda the good witch's melodic "to do's" and those funny little munchkins, terrorized by the bad witches (one crushed, leveled), singing and dancing about their productivity.

One of my assessment questions for many who fall into this Midwestern Farm Workers Union (it probably actually exists!) is, "Do you like to take baths?"

This reveals a person's capacity to relax. You'd be surprised; people who don't even know they have an issue with relaxing can't hide from the bath question. I remember in my very distant past, taking a bath and thinking, *What the heck am I going to do in here for the next ten minutes?* It was sheer torture. I actually bought a hot tub to "cure" myself of this issue—it worked! For the mourner or griever, this could be a triple-whammy. We are a part of the union, are grieving, and could have post-traumatic stress.

And I forgot about the part where we might be a woman. Women are biologically engineered and socialized "to do." One could argue that men are also; after all, they define themselves by what they do—or have.

We women do the opposite. We silently do and don't ask for credit. In fact, we dummy down to make others comfortable. This is deeply ingrained in women's constitution. (These are generalizations, of course.) Ultimately, I believe who we are is not defined by what we do or what we have.

Now I am looking at my grief response, my PTSD, as it is reflected in my moves. The ultimate "to do." I have perpetually loved looking for new places to live—countries, states, towns, houses, and even apartments. When I see a for-sale sign, I spend more than a glance, examining what's behind the sign. I'm adventurous and curious by nature. And a gambler. A risk-taker, to a point. These qualities could mask underlying issues. I am now conscious of this behavior, though, and am committed to never moving again. Well, never say never.

As we were settling in to our new community, I began to see this manifest in another potentially harmful direction. Something much more immediate. Something much more of an escape. Something that had the potential to bind me in the shame cycle, good and tight. It was the ultimate new place, in this new town—the biggest little city with the biggest escape route (move) I've ever known. I'm talking about casinos. The ultimate "move." When you are in a casino, you could be anywhere in the world. Oh boy, is there a lot "to do" in a casino. *And I did it all!*

Ding, Ding, Ding, Ding, Ding

Ding (v.): to dwell on with tiresome repetition or reiteration

I weep alone. I've talked about the behaviors we use to avoid our loneliness, our anxieties, and our sad feelings. My grief. Well, I hit the jackpot when we moved to Nevada. And it came out of nowhere.

When my parents suggested we check out Reno, Nevada, we were amused. "Like that's gonna happen," we secretly giggled. This town never crossed our minds, because ignorantly, we didn't have a clue about it. We had made a right turn from the California Bay area to Lake Tahoe for twenty years but had never seen Reno, another thirty miles east. In an effort to indulge my family, we checked it out. And we were hooked. We were coming from a small town that was beginning to feel like an island. We spent most of our weekends and vacations in Tahoe, and the travel was getting old. Though I thought we knew the "ding, ding, ding, ding, ding," it didn't factor into the equation, one way or another. We had other considerations. In our minds, we were looking for a change, wanted to be close to family, and loved the Sierras—the lake, the skiing, and the grand and heavenly outdoors. (Remember, I was completely unconscious about my double-whammy grief losses.) When we were looking for houses, we often stayed in a casino hotel. And the sound of the "ding, ding, ding, ding, ding" fluttering through my mind was torturous as I was trying to sleep.

In our first six months in Reno, we had a constant flow of visitors. Sheets and towels. Sheets and towels. We had four weekends in six months when there *weren't* any visitors. People came out of the woodwork. As my husband and I were waiting to get our new state professional licenses, and we had money set aside from our real estate sale, we welcomed everyone.

"Come see the lake; come ski; come camp, hike, bike, trike. Whatever."

Whatever. Well, they came. And we ended up in the casinos, each and every time. This was not just about our guests but also of our own volition. In our naïveté, we got completely sucked in. In one week, in the first month, I hit three separate jackpots. Wow! It was magic. (I hardly kidded myself that *I* was magic, just lucky.) And it was great fun. And then there were the comps. The fabulous "free" meals at the steakhouse. The spa. And the hosts. We had one host who figured out we had a toddler and asked us if we wanted tickets to *Sesame Street Live*. We were impressed. And completely inexperienced. It was like our own country club, and we were special. (I now equate casino hosts to an actor's agent—we became like a form of property.)

Now, don't get me wrong. We had been to Vegas, once every couple of years, but hardly gambled. We walked the strip and enjoyed the pools, restaurants, art, and shows. My belief was that gambling was a waste of money. (I'd been conservative with my money. I'm a saver of sorts. And I don't care for clutter, so I'm not a big spender.) And inevitably, we wasted money in Vegas if we gambled. I thought everybody lost when they gambled. I'd never hit a jackpot in my life, probably because I'd played a quarter at a time. I'd also been to the casino near my parents' home with my brother, when we were all together, visiting during holidays. He and I played blackjack. Again, I'd play the least dollar value I could and stop when I'd lost forty dollars. (My brother was another story.) It was just something "to do."

The Good Luck Fisherwoman

Luck (n.): a force that brings good fortune or adversity

My best friend, Scott, and I had been to Vegas four times before he got sick. It was our annual trip without our partners. It was so much fun with him; he gambled nickels, and I gambled quarters, but we mostly people-watched. I have great memories of these times, but none involved the actual gambling (well, maybe once, when Scott screamed from the other side of the room because he won four hundred nickels. This amused and embarrassed me to no end).

As my husband and I were slowly—or perhaps rapidly—being seduced by our new "country club," I was beginning my first dance with compulsivity. I didn't see it coming. I'd been so vigilant in my life. And I was health conscious. While I was in the casino, I remember having thoughts about addiction, about adrenaline, about "what if I run into a Napa client?" (I hadn't opened my new practice in Reno yet.) Shame.

How likely was it I would run into a Napa client? This reveals the depth of my shame. I remember having hideous thoughts. After all, the casino may have been our new country club, but for me, that included drinking, smoking, and gambling. I had been a "social" smoker some of my life; I'd smoke with others who smoked. Well, nothing like a casino for an opportunistic smoker!

It was ironic because in high school and some of college, I hung out with the smokers but didn't smoke. As a theatre major, smoking was all around me. I thought it was disgusting. My mom's secondhand smoke in the car, with the windows rolled up, left me an anti-smoker. Somewhere along the line, this began to change. In my twenties, if I went out drinking with friends, I inevitably smoked. Naturally, I've analyzed this to death. I've concluded it was the "if you can't fight them, join them" idea. Obviously, there's more to this story.

I would have periods—years—where I never touched a cigarette. And then, some circumstance, like a vacation, would come up. I still was vigilant, however, and would not become a daily smoker. At some point, in those early years, I wanted to figure this out. It just didn't fit in with the picture I saw of myself. There also was the shame and my belief that this behavior made me inauthentic. (My authentic self was healthy.) And the children around me were taught that only bad people smoked, which was unbearable—and so not right. I sought out hypnotherapy to help kick the habit. A guided visualization. The short answer: smoking was a connection to my mom. (Another unhelpful gift that left me angry.)

Well, there is no way I could tolerate being in a casino and not smoke. Not because of willpower but rather, I couldn't put up with the smoke around me unless I was smoking. I don't know how people do it. And I do like to smoke. Except for the stink. And the cancer. And the respiratory distress. And how I'd feel the next day.

And then, there are the free drinks at the casino. And if you are a special member of the country club, you get fabulous wine. I'm one of those people who will make the most out of a given situation. Freebies. The freebie here was Rombauer chardonnay—my favorite. As an adult child of an alcoholic, I had to monitor my intake. This was tricky when offered free Rombauer, and I was possibly making up for my losses. I'd drink wine, and then I'd drink water. Wine, water, wine, water, and so forth. Watching the clock and keeping track, or so I told myself.

As an ACoA who acquired a taste and appreciation for wine, having lived in the Napa Valley, I had certain rules for my life. I would not drink liquor (except for times like a margarita in Mexico, or a Rumrunner in Florida—vacation exceptions). My husband hardly drinks, so we have very old unopened bottles of liquor in our house; we aren't even sure how we acquired them. But a wine rule (drinking only wine) in no way negates the potential for alcoholism. Nothing can. Eventually, I had the same rules for smoking. If I was going to smoke, it was American Spirits, the "healthier" brand. Hah! No matter how badly I wanted a cigarette, I was never going to stoop to Marlboro Greens.

But the gambling. The jackpots. The adrenaline. That was the killer. The flush of shame I would experience after what seemed like a long night would leave me ruminating for days. And nights. Even when I would leave with loads of money. I had one experience where I hit ten thousand dollars, the highest jackpot on the machine. It was really fun at the time. And then, the adrenaline headache, which I experienced for five days, made it impossible for me to ever walk past that machine again.

The relentless rumination occurred because my behavior in the casino was so unlike me, and the unhealthiness of it all really affected my picture of myself. This was intolerable. It was rarely about the waste of money; more the waste of time. And the drinking, smoking, and gambling. And I would process it to death with my friends in my inner circle. I would analyze it. I found it fascinating, as a therapist, who had worked with compulsive behaviors for years, that I hadn't felt the grip before.

My ACoA would surface, and I'd start setting policy. We could only do it on the weekend. We could only do it if someone was in town and wanted to go. The trouble was the comps. (Comps are points you build up that give you the free meals, free tickets, free other things.) And we knew it, yet it was irresistible. We would end up back in the casino, for a "free" pedicure or a meal, and it would start all over again. I know this is typical. I've heard many stories of people who drive all over town for their ten-dollar free play.

Luckily, I was building a practice in Reno. And though I would share some of my experience with certain clients, when it was appropriate, I was terrified I'd run into someone in the casino. Drinking, smoking, gambling—not a good thing for a client to witness. And the shame had the potential to keep me up at night, yet I continued to engage with it.

And I was a lucky gambler—most of the time. (Obviously the key is to leave when you are ahead. You do anything for too long or too much, and bad things happen.)

I've always been a lucky person. When I was younger, I was called the "good luck fisherwoman." If you were fishing next to me, you could catch a forty-pound snook with an eight-pound line, though you may have difficulty landing it. My luck with gambling only made it worse. But the feeling of shame made it prohibitive.

I Might Not Be So Important

Might: used in auxiliary function to express permission, liberty, probability, or possibility in the past or present condition contrary to fact

When I would talk to my friends about my worry over being seen drinking, smoking, and gambling, they thought it was nonsense. Why was I so concerned? After all, in their minds, I was a person who really didn't care what people thought, and they believed my client's could not care less about my personal life. This included two friends who are therapists and two minister friends—not my consultants. At the time, I did not divulge this to my consultants--therapists or spiritual guides--because of the shame. And in my mind, my friends underestimated the power of the smoking shame. This was a biggy. The one that has become "You are a bad person if you smoke—at all. No matter what." I hear this all the time. And even though smoking was an intermittent casino activity, I was fearful of being "caught." It seemed so silly to my friends, but *so real* in my world. And probably for good reason. I would easily assume I would lose clients if they saw me at a casino.

Although it was a relief to think I might not be so important, I still knew I didn't care for this shameful feeling, and I wasn't used to it. I also believed this was not me—this person having fun, acting out, not caring. I was responsible, accountable, and good. Healthy. The teacher's pet. The well-behaved person. The dutiful daughter. The good therapist who would not engage in anything that was seemingly irresponsible, reckless, or inauthentic. So who was this gal? (Remember the ACoA definition number five: *ACoAs have difficulty having fun.*)

My double-whammy grief experience, when my brother and Scott died, changed my life, in that "caring what people think" way. I think everyone cares what other people think; it's only human (and possibly very female), but it's part of our natural development, as adults, is to shed this, decade by decade. In our twenties and thirties, we are building (this supports the "caring what people think" way). In our forties, our life is pretty full, with family, work, and other responsibilities. It's only natural we don't have as much room for those who are peripheral. We begin to care less about what other people think. In our fifties and sixties, we are losing people—parents, aunts and uncles. They naturally fall off the "caring what people think" list. In our seventies and eighties ... well, we all hope we will be elderly adults who don't give a sh**t what people think.

For me, following the loss of my brother and best friend, I jumped ahead to not caring what people think, to the degree that I could, being human (and a psychotherapist), of course. My double-whammy loss occurred when I was in my late thirties, so I skipped a few developmental hurdles. I watched the "caring what people think" bubble leave my mind and travel away. In an instant. Like watching a balloon released into the atmosphere. Very quickly, I couldn't see it anymore.

I immediately stopped making decisions that were not necessarily in my best interest; that were related to what I believed other people wanted. For instance, prior to my "caring what people think" balloon being released, I would drive six hours in blizzard conditions, usually a three-hour trip, for a quick weekend with my parents, whom I felt (my issue) needed to be with their grandchild. This was dangerous. I could have visited them two weeks later, when the weather was better. At the time, I could not see this as an option. It never occurred to me to put off the planned trip; I didn't want to disappoint. (I'm remembering a time when my son was two, and my hands were freezing as I put chains on my tires by myself in a nasty blizzard. *Eight years later*—the "caring what people think" balloon was released). My grief experience provided clarity for me. I'm sure, on some level, this also has to do with becoming more conscious about the preciousness of life. All I know is something shifted in me.

But this all was completely undone when the drinking, smoking, and gambling occurred.

The Pesky Parrot on Your Shoulder

Parrot (n): a person who sedulously echoes another's words

As I began analyzing my behavior, I naturally considered addiction. Though I was never going to lose everything to this country club, I had to contemplate my actions. I'm a therapist, after all. I've spent years talking about the shame that binds you. And here it was. And I have a lecturette I use, when talking about any compulsive behaviors, involving a parrot. It goes like this:

I rest my right hand against my right shoulder and say, "There is a parrot on your shoulder, who is there to help himself get whatever you are addicted to—shopping, the computer, alcohol, cocaine, gambling, moving. And until you realize he's taken over your voice, your 'self,' he is dictating your day, planning, manipulating, and controlling."

In psychology, there are many descriptions of this exact voice but I came up with the concept of a parrot and have used it for years. I like it, because parrots do sit on people's shoulders. They do speak. And they can be knocked off. Crushed. Leveled. You can get rid of them. And they can fly away. This is not your voice, but the voice of the critic—or the addict. And with one flick, he can be eliminated. Okay, maybe not quite so easily as that, but you can talk back to your parrot. You can have a conversation, an argument. You can have a new thought, one that destroys or replaces the previous thought. And you can cut off communication. In my analysis, I started wondering if I had a parrot on my shoulder. Was I an addict? (You can see why this might have become intolerable.)

I remember when my brother was in the throes of his addiction, and we would talk about his process. He believed I could never understand. And I couldn't. He loved to romanticize and philosophize about it. (This was just another aspect of his parrot.) He looked at his forays into the worst and most dangerous parts of whatever city (to buy his crack cocaine) as a sociology project. Again, the parrot—manipulating, planning, and romanticizing. At the time, in my meager attempt to relate, I could only mention smoking. There were those times when I made a choice that I believed was about being with friends, but ultimately, I wondered if it was all about smoking. When I agreed to party in a way or at a place where I knew I could end up smoking, was my parrot planning the whole thing? Was my parrot exercising her need for a cigarette under the guise of a party? This is typical codependent overanalysis. I truly doubt I spent time with friends in order to smoke, but you never know. These are powerful unconscious urges. This, of course, offers no comparison to a crack addiction. And his romanticism sickened me. These conversations never lasted long.

Today, if I were to have a similar discussion with my brother, I would share that during those early casino days, I fantasized and thought seriously about writing a documentary on the casino world. The rituals I observed intrigued me. (I loved this!) There were people who thought they were "slot machine whisperers." I observed the belief systems. The weirdos. The predators. The competition. The whole game. Though I think there's an interesting story to be told, one could argue that this was my parrot, romanticizing.

Again, as I watched my seduction into the gambling arena, I wondered about my own parrot. Every time I set a parameter or boundary and then made a pedicure appointment in the salon at the casino, I listened and listened for this voice—the voice I'd talked about for so many years with my friends and clients. I'd search for the moment I went unconscious. The moment my mind wandered to video poker. Was it the day I made the appointment or even before? It was easy to argue with the parrot; after all, you can get a pedicure on any corner. But this one was free. Hah! And then I'd watch my impulsivity—the excitement I felt walking through the casino to my appointment upstairs, glancing at the machines to see what the progressive (a jackpot that fluctuates in dollar amounts) was up to. And my thoughts, while I was relaxing into my pedicure, were on what was happening downstairs. And then there was my choice to sit down and play poker. My heart demonstrated the adrenaline stress. I worried like crazy about my health. And the duality—the shame and guilt. I checked my phone, my watch—and again, my pulse.

My parrot had won. And then I'd go home, eat well, do my yoga, and play with my kids and my animals. And try like hell to forget about it.

Heal Thy Diagnostic Self

Self (n.): the union of elements as body, emotions, thoughts, and sensations that constitute the individuality and identity of a person

As time went on, the policies were helping, yet the ante (not so much literally) was being raised. I was suddenly in high limits. You can hide there more easily. We were spending less time at the casino and had many rules about it, yet I still felt shame about going. At the same time, we were beginning to create a life in Reno. We were skiing two or three times a week. We would go to the lake for most weekends, hiking, biking, and kayaking. We were meeting people outside of the casino. (In that first year, our social life solely was through my family and friends we knew at the casino.) My daughter was finally in a setting where we could meet others. There is a real division in Reno between who goes to the casinos and who doesn't. And I desperately wanted to be on the "who doesn't" side. The shame was too much. Let me be clear: this is not a judgment on anyone who gambles or enjoys casinos. This is my issue. While I have fun (and I really did), my issues, my childhood ACoA issues, ruled out any chance of its remaining fun—at that time.

While going to the casino was not a regular event, by the end of that first year it was still feeling very unhealthy and shameful. It did not matter if I was "up" or "down"; it wasn't about the money—it was about the fact that I was doing something—drinking, smoking, and gambling—that made me feel bad about myself. Thus, it messed with my authentic-self notion—who I thought I was. As I began to unravel this tangled web, I was well aware of how it had become tangled, but I wondered about the why. Why, after all of these years, did I get sucked into this arena? It was so unlike me. I was the last person in my family who would waste money, waste time, and hide out, or engage in something unhealthy. So why now? How did I not see this coming?

As I began this journey of examination, some things stood out in my mind. My brother, Doug, and my best friend, Scott. And their deaths. And my subsequent move. My hypnotherapy and training had taught me about associations. I began investigating this. My only previous fun with casinos and gambling involved these two persons. (And then there is my husband, who, coincidentally, naturally hides out. He's an introvert, an identical twin, and has hearing loss. His internal life is vast.) These two losses devastated me. My brother Doug, Scott, and I had practically lived together in Ohio, New York, and California. My husband was just developing a relationship with my brother Doug when he died—they would have been great friends—and my husband never had the chance to meet Scott. Yet my husband reminds me so much of both of them, in the "funny, handsome charmer" kind of way. All three of them are characters—the kind you want to be around because you feel good in their presence.

When I met my husband the second time (we'd had a friendship before and then lost touch), I was grieving and very PTSD-symptomatic. Scott was withering away. And Doug was sucking away any last bit of energy I had. I was frantic to save them both. My husband was a godsend. I had literally asked God (this was intention work) to send him to me, just two weeks before he showed up. (I was specific and used his name—"a guy like Rich"—though I never expected to see him again; he had moved away.) He came back into my life just two months before Scott's last breath. And

I remember feeling very afraid to love him. He was too much like Scott and Doug. How could I risk losing him too? Don't these things come in threes? Yet, I had prayed for him for a long time. And here he was. He held me through the most difficult days and months.

I'll never forget his shell-shocked face when I came home one winter's day. I found multiple cars in the driveway—a scary and historically dreaded sight—although no one was supposed to be home yet. I thought my husband was with my son at his guitar lesson. Why was he here? Why were my best friends here?

I flew in the door without fear, only frustration, "What are you doing here? Where is Bjorn? What happened to his lesson?"

The idea that something was seriously wrong was far from my mind. But the control freak in me was alive and well. And then I got the familiar feeling—shivers. I quickly shifted gears as I took in my husband's forlorn face, and he began to tell me that the Marin County coroner's office had called. I immediately thought something had happened to one of my sisters who also lived in that county. My brother was still far from any of the rapid-fire thoughts racing through my mind, even though the idea he could die was solidified in my brain.

After the heavy-duty drama in our initial stages of our relationship (Scott's death and my brother's addiction and subsequent death), I knew my husband must love me (and that was important, with my having abandonment issues—trust is tenuous). However, I was deathly afraid to love him back. I was constantly waiting for the other shoe to drop. For the third loss. But my husband is kind of irresistible, so I took the plunge.

Another interesting factor, my husband's parents both love to gamble. He had been around it his whole life. He could easily have fun gambling with forty dollars on a penny machine. I, on the other hand, became obsessed with hitting jackpots.

Oh, My Gentle German

Gentle (adj.): suited to a person of high social station

How my wonderful husband fits into this picture is classic, in the ACoA/enabler scenario and, perhaps, in the Bavarian way. Now remember, I chose not to do research for this book, so this is my intuition and opinion. Before I met my husband, I knew only a little about Germans. And that mostly was what everyone thinks they know. What I didn't know is that they are fairly conflict avoidant—this is my assumption. My husband is a first- and second-generation German. My daughter has his beautiful sparkling blue eyes, and his difficult thin hair. His dad is lovely, funny, and kind (as was his mom before she passed)—and full of fear and paranoia. (The world is not a safe place, and people are out to get you.)

This is diametrically opposed to my own constitution, where the universe provides and keeps me safe. For example, one time when all of the brothers were over, we ordered pizza. When it arrived, it was burned. I suggested we call and ask for a new one. They believed the staff would just spit on the next one if we complained. I tried to explain to my husband that the chef would want to know if he was sending out an unacceptable product. Wouldn't we all? Don't we all want feedback? Ah, herein lies the dilemma.

What is feedback? What is criticism? What is constructive? What is conflict? And do all these roads lead to problems? Dead ends? Road blocks? *Hurt?* There are a lot of little secrets in my husband's family. Like many families. The kind where too many people know. And to me, they are not a big deal, but since they exist, they are imposing. I'm terrified I'll blurt something out and all hell will break loose and it'll be *all my fault*, even though I had nothing to do with it initially. Secrets are not uncommon in families. Yet for me, a secret keeper by profession, I can't handle so many secrets in my personal life. It leads to inauthenticity.

My husband and I have worked on this since day one. (This is on the list of ACoA stuff I gave him when we met.) Tell the truth; it's good enough. Why lie when you don't have to? It's like living a double life, and everybody knows it. It's a shame piece. Why do we need a better excuse or explanation than the one we have, the truthful one? You can see how this may add to my already complex picture of guilt and shame around the gambling. And if my husband is conflict avoidant, then how does he assert himself around this? Naturally, because I'm a therapist, we have had numerous discussions about this. I don't let anything go. Poor man. And it's not easy, but I'm terribly afraid of being one of those couples that wakes up years later, full of resentment, because somebody didn't say something. I want all things said. And I pretty much say all things. I think I can take it. I hope so.

What conflict-avoidant people don't understand is that it is difficult being the assertive one—otherwise known as the control freak. It is burdensome; wracked with responsibility and therefore, accountability. We (control freaks) have to make all of the decisions and live with the consequences. It'd be nice to hand that over. To sit back and let things happen, rather than being the one who makes things happen. But I understand that it's a complex crystal, full of variables created long before we even met.

This dynamic came up during this time when my husband or I would suggest that we go out, which became code for going to the casino—and the other would enable. I'd set the rules, and we'd break them together.

In the early days of this adventure, our issues (my ACoA, his conflict avoidance, and the possibility of our potential for addictive personalities) would sabotage my policies. For instance, let's say I had a rule about no gambling during the week. I'd come home from a busy and stressful day at my practice, and my husband would say, "Want to go out?"

I'd already been thinking about this after my last client. (Or was this my parrot, planning?) But I'd say, "No, honey, it's a school night." Then the guilt would set in and the codependent would arrive (and I'd done a lot of work in this area). Minutes later, I'd say, "Well, okay, if you want, but only for a little while."

And boom—we were on our way.

The ultimate move.

I Choose God over Google

Over (prep.): used as a function word to indicate superiority, advantage, or preference

It's been interesting, living among these New York Germans. And enjoyable. They are a lively bunch, just as my Boston Scottish family can be. And I'm not certain these fearful characteristics are regional, international, or just psyche related. All I know is that it's a completely different reality than my own. And my spiritual beliefs are resolute. I've always felt blessed by my unshakable belief that the universe (God) sustains me. And I've felt sorry for those who don't know what this is like—to know this. It has truly saved my life. It's knowing that whatever happens, it will be okay. For this I am grateful. (This is especially handy during late-night ruminations.)

Not too long ago, my father-in-law was visiting. He caught me at the right time. I'd been contemplating this world we live in. This Google world. I'd turned on the television to catch something my clients referred to and was struck by how many talk shows are on in the afternoon. And by talk shows, I include *The Doctors, Dr. Oz*—the ones that are about health, which I believe are seemingly helpful but ultimately hurtful. Most of these shows basically tell you there is something wrong with you, whether it's your décor or your heart. The potential for disaster is looming. (I don't include *Ellen* in here; to me, she is sheer joy and intentionally provides this.)

My father-in-law had remarked several times, "You should Google …"

I finally said to him, "Pops, I choose God over Google." And I explained, "You live in this world of fear and anxiety, a reality you create and validate through your news, radio, and computer. I can't live there. I have enough natural anxiety. I choose my reality to be God, where love resides. This is my working reality."

And I meant it. This has always been my reality. Even in the toughest of times, I can rely on love. My own loving nature. I see beauty in everything. I'm the perpetual observer. I can't help myself. And I have compassion for all situations. I understand why people do bad things—they are in a hell of a lot of pain. And to me, hell is a state of mind. Just as heaven is. When you are in mental hell, you do bad things. When you are in a heavenly state of mind, you come from a loving place and do good works. This is in my constitution. I believe wholeheartedly in loving, first and foremost. And when this is tested at times, I work like mad to come from a loving place. To seek first to understand. And usually, the answer is pain. Pain is in the middle of the difficult situation. Mine or theirs. And when I can't understand, and there are those times when I can't, I steer clear.

And I'm very clear on the why.

Kick the Clique

Clique (n): one held together by a presumed identity of interests views, or purposes

I mentioned that I was very involved in my Napa Center for Spiritual Living before my double-whammy grief experience. When we were considering moving to Reno, we checked out the demographics. Nevada seemed a little scary, in an inexplicable kind of way, but we found out great things—amazing amounts of cultural options. Incredible summers and winters. Easy airport access. And any shop you could possibly need. And a large metaphysical community, beyond the three metaphysical churches (maybe even more). This was unbelievable. And it solidified our move. The idea that there were like-minded people living here sealed the deal.

When we arrived, we attended the church nearest our house. It was all delightfully familiar and affirming. The size of the church was overwhelming, as compared to my Napa church, and I couldn't make any connections. I attributed this to "cliquishness," which I believed to be a reality in this new town. Years later, when I mentioned this to my minister, she shared a fable about a person who arrives in a new town and sees what she wants to see. She gets what she asks for.

This person in the new location asks an elder, "What kind of town is this?"

And the elder replies, "What was it like in the town you came from?"

I know these laws, these universal conditions. It was a good story, and I thought about it, yet it was hard to see myself in it. I don't remember ever thinking Napa was a cliquish town. And I still don't.

I think, now, that my inability to connect or feel a part of the church was a further demonstration of my guilt and shame over what was going on elsewhere. At my "country club." As an ACoA and a therapist and a natural metaphysician, I couldn't tolerate the hypocrisy. How could I go to church, knowing I was engaging in behaviors that were blocking me from my highest good? And aren't country clubs full of cliques? Hmmm. I decided to kick the clique—the notion of it, that is.

I started church shopping. I was raised by two Unitarians and am proud of it. There were lots of options for me here. But then, this was a family affair. Compromise. For my husband, church begins in September and ends on Super Bowl Sunday. Actually, his beliefs are akin to transcendentalism, an antecedent to Unitarianism. He would say that his God is in nature, akin to Henry David Thoreau and Ralph Waldo Emerson, a Unitarian minister. My metaphysics, though a new language, was something he could embrace and understand. These movements are evolutionary and culminate in New Thought. In my efforts to connect, I took classes. I attended edifying lectures. This involved loads of reading and self-examination. And, thank goodness, awakening. I'd done this before, but it's always a fresh experience or process when we are with new people or in new classes. Don't ever discount this—the energy of a classroom of bright minds.

I also believe this word *clique*, this feeling of being on the outside, is old, unpleasant, and familiar. I believe I would do anything to avoid the feelings it brings up. Yet there are times when I still struggle with this, because of my "caring what people think" balloon. Yet I work hard on maintaining my boundaries and being clear on my and my family's needs. I don't want to waste a minute of my life being in a situation I would rather not be in, after losing so many, so young.

Perhaps Napa didn't feel cliquish because I had my own clique there. And maybe the acceptance of being in that clique contributed to my move. Did I deserve these dear friends and success? I don't really believe this, but I had a good group of friends in Napa and a contented life. However, two of those people who were my constants (for better or for worse) are now dead. Though they were not from or living in Napa, the evidence is pretty clear.

In Reno, I initially struggled to find genuine friendships (this goes straight to the idea of authenticity). I believe this was because I was hiding out. Isolating. Because of my shame. (And because of my profession— anonymity was necessary, in my mind. Certainly a good thing as a therapist in a small town.) Perhaps that was one of the draws of the casino world. After all, I've referred to it as a country club; you are made to feel like a special, chosen member. You find yourself talking to almost anyone, because you have no defenses, no discernment, and because you are unconscious. Meaning, you are not truly present. And you are in the clique, so you can hide.

In high school, I was voted Most Likely to Nonconform (and Most Likely to Get Married). One, I was proud of; the other, not so much (see how I put it in parens.) I came to a prestigious prep school through the courts. There were custody issues, personality struggles, and the guardian ad litem recommended boarding school. Though I ended up not boarding, I found myself in a very cliquish world. Bloomfield Hills, Michigan, holds one of those statistics, like "most money per square mile per something per something." This began my journey into the world of cliques. Prior to this, I was a team player—literally, on many swim teams and thus, relays. And I continued in high school theatre and a madrigal group. Because of the dysfunction in my family, though, I felt alone and different. I think I may have looked and sounded all right.

Looking back, high school just seems like a dream. I can't relate to the nightmare most refer to; I wasn't even there, mentally and emotionally. I never skipped a day; I had more serious issues to contend with, like survival. The jungle that defines high school for most was my oasis away from the jungle of my life.

I know this notion that I somehow kicked the clique was empty. (I think it's pretty hard to disabuse us of a notion.) This clique wound was and probably still is alive and well and living in every corner of my unconscious. I know this because at times, it continues to kick me in my rear. And I never see it coming. Denial—oh, how I love it. I worship the idea that ignorance is bliss.

I've never been good at denial, so when it surfaces, I luxuriate in it, though it never lasts long enough—because then comes the beating. Yes, these lessons arrive by a swift and hard-hitting backhand (as they often do), after I've already been through nine rounds. It usually involves family situations where I set a limit, a boundary, and there is resistance. And although I am thankful for it at the time, it still digs up old feelings of abandonment and loss. (I am out of the clique, even though it is my choice.) And stubborn me, I wrestle with it and hold on to the struggle and hurt, until I can no longer. It's like I'm ready to jump out of the helicopter for my freedom, and instead, I find myself hanging on the platform with one arm, and I won't let go, even though I know I have a parachute. And a backup. There is an incontrovertible parachute in my world, because it's never failed me. It can't. The universe. God. My true authentic self.

And when I finally let go, the universe envelopes me, and I get the greatest perspective—crystal clear. And it's all okay. Better than okay, because it certainly wasn't okay during the beating. I wasn't seeing things clearly, and that's why I found myself holding on and feeling bad. Because I was in denial. I was holding onto an old idea, a false notion. A notion about belonging.

After these heart-wrenching days, I've often found myself saying to the universe, "Oh! I get it now. You were trying to tell me to ..."

And then I go through the litany of self-criticism, which goes like this: "How did I not see this coming? All of the signs were there."

This usually involves boundaries in my case, as I suspect it does for most. And though it wasn't any fun getting there, the epiphany is worth it. The lesson was learned, and I survived the process. I feel intense relief. Free. And I belong where I am meant to be.

Thank God.

PART 3

OH GREAT GOD!

Grazing and Gazing

I n my life, I have cultivated and managed a spiritual practice for as long as I can remember. I believe this consciously began around age nine. Nine is a magical age for most girls, as it is the time in our life where we can be a boy and a girl at the same time. We can shed our princess and climb trees, ride bikes, and play in creeks, without any hint of the gender pressures sure to arrive in the coming years.

My clear first memory of God was a day when I needed to get away from the chaos of my home. Things were beginning to unravel in my family, and I hopped on my bicycle and crossed the very busy street we lived on, riding to the Methodist church parking lot on the other side. Alongside this church and parking lot was a large, open, weed-ridden field. I loved the humps and bumps of my bike on this field, as it transformed me to another place and time. My handlebars became the mane of my horse. My seat, the hard-ridden saddle. The ground, my grand prairie. I never noticed the tract of homes nearby. Just the croaking ponds. And the whispering willows. And the glorious sky. This is where I felt connected to something greater; naturally, with the sky. (After all, isn't that where God resides?) Even as a nine-year-old, I knew the universe sustained me and made everything else feel better or vanish. It was just me, my horse, and my God.

I was safe.

Many years later, when I came home from school on senior-ditch day (which I did for the very first time), I was already feeling shameful, as I'd had a great, fun day, hanging out with people I'd not been comfortable around previously and had been a "bad girl." I came home at what I thought was the most opportune time to avoid being seen. Instead, there were several cars in our driveway, including the car belonging to my brother, who we hadn't heard from in a while. And my older sister's car (she was away at college). This was puzzling. I felt shivers dancing up and down my spine and entered the house, wondering what the hell was going on. Surely they couldn't all be here over my skipping school. How could they even know? Was it really that big a deal? No. It wasn't.

But the death of my mom was, indeed.

My family had gathered to inform us that my mom was found dead by the police, after her friendly postman had noticed her mail piling up. She had died on Mother's Day, two days prior. I had had rough dealings with my mom in the days leading up to Mother's Day; she'd seemed delusional and scary. At this point, most of my experiences with her were unsettling in the "Oh, my God, who are you, and why do I have to deal with this?" sort of way. And I did what most teenagers would do (though I clearly wasn't most teenagers): I sought refuge in the arms of my boyfriend.

When I heard the words, "Your mother has died," I knew nothing except I couldn't breathe. And I needed a quick and easy escape. I swiftly slipped into the garage, onto my bike, and off I went. I doubt anyone noticed. I rode and rode and rode. I couldn't tell you where. I couldn't tell you how, but somewhere and somehow, I ended up in the van of my boyfriend's soccer team—unglued, defenseless, sweaty, tear-stained, and exhausted. And embarrassed. I guess they took me home. And the next day, I went to school. My vice principal pulled me aside and told me to go home. I couldn't go home; I had skipped school the day before and *my mother was found dead*. And my father and stepmother sent me to school that next day, probably thinking it would keep me distracted.

I remember walking torpidly around the lovely campus of my beautiful, prominent high school (Kingswood School Cranbrook), studying my physical surroundings. I had felt unbelievably blessed to be at this school, an outsider from another world. I was sure I was one of the few who appreciated its awesomeness. Most of the student body lived nearby, and I assumed they probably took it for granted. I sat down by the sweet little lake and started picking blades of grass. I love to pull the blade in such a perfect way as to achieve the greatest level of edible parts—the white. Yes, I starting eating grass. Somewhere between the grass, the lake, the sky, and the "hearty meal," I was comforted. I took it all in. And after a sufficient amount of grazing and gazing, I began the arduous many-mile walk to my childhood best friend's house, where I knew I would be welcomed.

The Camel and the Tent

When I was twelve, I left my family of origin to live with my oldest friend's family. We'd been best friends since first grade. This was a result of my mother's alcoholism and my father's being a workaholic. My father's work helped him escape the pandemonium of home. Things were falling apart. My brother and I had a car accident. Doug drove us into a ditch while backing out of our driveway. He was thirteen and a half or so and was driving me to my piano lesson. This was not an uncommon scenario. We pretty much did what we needed to. My neighbor and good family friend was called, and she immediately took in my younger sister. The rest of us went with our close friends. (I think my older sister was already living with her friend.) Mine was a home I knew well. My friend's mom, the one I went to live with, had an alcoholic mother and had shared her sympathetic story with me many times. It was so helpful and reassuring to know she knew what it was like. Maybe I would be okay. I had been a part of this family for years.

This was the beginning of my moves.

At first, I slept on the couch in their living room, just feet from the front door. I remember being terrified that someone would come through that door. Someone scary. I recall exercising in that living room, trying to bulk up in case I needed to be strong. Sit-ups, push-ups—it was a sixth grade mentality in 1976. I also remember feigning illness whenever they went out to dinner, not wanting to further my existing burden on them, being another mouth to feed. When this family moved, they built a new house with a bedroom for me. I had a new family! It was a dream come true—until theirs fell apart. Divorce. And completely unexpected—to me anyway. This was about the time a custody battle began between my parents. And Kingswood School was brought into the mix because it was a boarding school. I was terrified of this school--especially the idea of boarding. In the end, for various reasons, I found friends where I could reside.

From there, I ended up living with many different families (including my own) over the course of middle school and high school. I believe there were six families in all. (I think I bounced around, not wanting to overstay my welcome and being torn about my friendships.) One of these families, a wonderful and stable family, was first generation American from Palestine. I remember the mom, who was beautiful and cosmopolitan--a dream for any ACoA—kidding me about how I was like a camel who stuck its nose in the tent, as if to ask, "Can I come in?" I'm sure I laughed at the time, though now it feels sad. And this many years later, I well up when I think of it. I am no camel.

And then I attached myself to my high school boyfriend's family. They were Italian and offered the splendor of the embrace of an Italian family. I loved them. They seemed to have it all together. And they took me in as one of their own. I was lucky that way. Even when I ran away to England in my junior year to a boarding school, I ended up living with my English boyfriend's family. And I fell in love with them. This was my first of three transcontinental moves. And you know the rest of the story. This is where and why it all began. My many moves.

The Ties That Bind

As I refer to my shameful gambling period, I'm actually acknowledging that this final move to Nevada, to this new state and this casino fun, only opened the door for the work to come through. The work I needed to do. The unresolved grief work that was apparently oozing out for many years. It was the final piece of ACoA work (to date), which was about authenticity.

In my life, I'd done a lot of psychological work on my own—don't try this at home—as well as spiritual work. I try to be a better person, to stay on a path of growth and transformation and intelligence. I believe God (a spiritual practice) is all there is, and what we need. I believe God/ Spirit is love (not a man in the sky with a white beard making decisions). I avoid toxic people. I avoid people who drain me. I've learned to maintain boundaries where they are concerned. This can be lonely but in the end, all we have is our relationship with our true self. This is what I believe. Yes, we have our great loves, our family, yet ultimately, we have ourselves.

Trust begins and ends with our selves. And the only other relationship we can truly count on is with God—our inner spiritual being—and of course the outer, which is everywhere.

Though I feel lonely at times, I have so much intimacy in my life that it all seems okay. I know I want and nurture authentic connections, those where I can be myself, completely free of judgment. Or baloney. I don't want to waste my time with others. This is not to say I don't enjoy peripheral relationships; of course I do. I just seek and hope to practice authenticity in them as well, when it is safe—when I am with persons who are also practicing authenticity.

I look at my relationship history and my pattern. In my early years, I left any time I felt abandoned by grief or loss. I also put up with many toxic people. After my "caring what people think" bubble drifted away, I no longer tolerated the people in my life who were depleting me. Of course, there are those we must acquaint ourselves with for the sake of family peace, but there are some family members with whom I have severed ties.

In my practice, this comes up now and then, when there is a toxic family member—a discussion about how to cope. For some reason, we're indoctrinated to believe we have to put up with this person. I believe blood doesn't mean bound, even though we have phrases like "blood is thicker than water," "the tie that binds," and "but he is my family." These are mixed messages, all endorsing our belief that we have to deal with the person, regardless, because we are biologically related.

I ask my clients and friends, "Would you walk in a room where a flea bomb was just released?" No. You would not. "This particular relative is a poison, and being near a poison makes you sick. It could possibly kill you or break your spirit."

With clients, I tend to preface these talks with, "Remember, we hold that your mom and dad, or other, did the best they could with what they had—'had' being physically, psychologically, or spiritually—and we still need to look at where the gaps are, for it is in these gaps that the healing takes place."

It's a tricky navigation.

At one point, I was running a day-treatment program for adolescents. Some were very angry. Some had committed brutal acts. I remember being impressed by this; it was so foreign to me. I remember examining my life and my avoidance of anger, especially where my mother was concerned. This was before Scott and Doug had died. And my brother's death brought up anger in a big way.

While I never severed my tie with my brother, I did abandon the hope that I could rescue him. I thought I had done it, though this book has forced me to question this. I now believe my anger towards him after his death was my way of coping with the fact that I didn't save him. That I couldn't save him. My ultimate heartbreak. After many years of wrenching rescue attempts, which included numerous welfare checks, day-treatment visits, and many types of Something Anonymous meetings, the final blow was at his last treatment program, where I had him in my county, and I had loads of connections.

I pleaded, "If I can just keep him in this county, I can save his life."

He quickly moved in with a woman he had met prior to the treatment, through a misdial to his drug dealer, two counties away—unbelievably, their relationship started accidentally, over the phone. And then, they both quickly left my county. And my hopes were dashed. Even though his move with his girlfriend provided loads up hope for my family, I knew better. First rule of recovery: no relationships for the first year. For good reason. I had very little support trying to enforce this rule. I was considered the bad cop and the doomsayer. I truly believed the only thing that would save my brother was incarceration, and I thought I could manage this in my county—again, with connections. And I was probably right.

I would tell my family, "I would rather have him behind bars than dead!"

Clearly, nobody thought it would come to that. My brother's charms and all-American attractiveness helped him escape situations that landed others in jail. Though I believe in treatment programs over incarceration (wholeheartedly), it wasn't working for him. He wasn't doing the work, the therapy—the place where we find out why we need to numb the pain. And its source.

Where I have severed a relationship, I have worked on forgiveness, for my own spiritual wellness. To me, forgiveness comes with an acknowledgement and apology. And I believe in this practice. We cannot truly forgive someone who doesn't acknowledge the harm and is not sorry. I no longer practice "forget-ness." This has led to trouble in my life. I used to forgive and forget (a typical codependent response). And the forgetting part would sneak up, come back, and bite me, causing further damage. The following, simply put, is what I share with my clients and friends:

"Forgiveness is about letting go. We don't hang on to negative feelings, because these tend to fester and can cause disease. There is nothing healthy about a grudge. Not forgetting is about boundaries. Do not forget. Use it as a live-and-learn lesson. Draw a clear and solid line, and don't erase it."

And then let it go.

The Menu at the Restaurant

As I was considering my ACoA piece of work, I was thinking a lot about my relationships—again! I remember when I moved to the West Coast from the East Coast, I was struck by people's independence, individuality, and selfishness. Remember, as a codependent, any action that is for your self seems selfish. One Friday night, I had plans with a girlfriend—dinner and a movie—who'd been born and raised in Berkeley.

I called her before I was leaving to say, "I'll be there in twenty minutes or so, depending on the traffic."

"Oh, can I take a raincheck?" she casually asked. "I don't really feel like it."

Feel like it?! What does that mean? I didn't know if I felt like it, either. I only knew we had plans, and I was going! But I only said, "Sure, no problem." I was reeling and thinking, *People on the West Coast are rude and self-absorbed.* I'm sure I wasted many mental hours wondering about this selfishness that night.

This was a great lesson for me. It was twenty-five years ago, and it took some years to get, but I refer to it often with clients. *The very idea that you could do or not do what you wanted.* I never knew what *I* wanted, just what others needed. Or what I perceived they needed.

I say, wholeheartedly and emphatically, "The first dilemma is figuring out *what* you want. Then *make sure* it's what you want"—This is the most difficult first task for a codependent—"Only *do* what you want. Or *ask* for what you want. You may not get it, but at least you know what it is, and you've expressed it."

And of course, there are those times where we have to do things we don't necessarily want to do—like visit the in-laws or go to obligatory events—because it is the right thing to do. People (myself included) with a tendency toward unhealthy codependency, to their detriment, do the right thing all the time.

One of my assessment tools in this arena is the menu in any restaurant.

I'll ask a client, "When you go to a restaurant, do you order what you want?"

This can be perplexing. There is often a pause.

"Do you order based on price?" I'll ask.

This can take some thought. "Make believe that price is not an issue, in this instance."

Again, a pause.

"Do you order after you've heard what everyone else is ordering, so you can accommodate?"

This is tricky and takes some contemplation; navigation. The typical action is, "Well, if he's having steak, I should have…"

Or, and this is one of the saddest questions I'll ask, "Do you order based on what other people are going to think of you?" For instance, do you think, "I should have salad because I'm overweight."

Or the opposite. "I should order pasta so they think I'm eating. And then I continuously move my food around on the plate to disguise my diet."

You'd be amazed at how much information is gleaned from this one activity. You'd be amazed by how often people don't order what they want.

Why was I not ordering the meal I wanted? Why was I not walking my walk? Was this all about my grief, my best friend and brother, my many life events involving tragedy? If I truly wanted this, then why wasn't I ordering it?

I have, jokingly and seriously, shared with clients and friends that this can run so deep, viscerally, that a perpetual codependent can drive through the Taco Bell and when asked, "Do you want hot or mild sauce?" their internal response is, "What does she need me to have?" This young stranger. It is that immediate and unreasonable—and in the case of a cashier at Taco Bell, this response could literally come back to burn you.

Just Do It

In my practice, I often think of the brilliance of that Nike campaign, *Just Do It*. Wouldn't it be magnificent if we could all *just do it*? Wouldn't it be wonderful if I could just tell all of my clients to *just do it*? Of course, I'm just kidding. Yet there are those times when it is confusing. Certainly during my period of drinking, smoking, and gambling, I was pondering this Nike campaign. I was pondering many things about myself, my family, my clients, and my world. I knew I needed to get back to a spiritual practice. I talked the talk, and I thought I walked the walk, but I hadn't been seeking community. I was isolating. And was I really walking the walk? I had stopped my meditative practice, yet it didn't seem like it at the time. I spent—and still spend—a lot of time in the quiet. And I wasn't doing yoga, which is also a good thing for me and helps me stay focused and centered and healthy.

I was off track. And I wasn't facing it. Yet I was judging myself nearly every hour of every day. And it had been many years since I'd experienced this feeling of unbalance. I wasn't used to it and it was leading me to feel like a hypocrite.

This was exactly what was feeding my false belief about authenticity. At the time, I wasn't seeing clients, yet I still felt shameful—inauthentic. It went beyond my professional life, as authenticity would. I had compassion for everyone else but me. And I preach compassion to my people, for themselves.

Remember, I live metaphysics. I absorbed every writer who made it his or her life's work to help others reach their full potential and live a good life. I had rabidly read the material of all who shared the same universal philosophy, because it informed what I innately knew to be true. It reinforced what I felt and knew as that nine-year-old on my bicycle. The universe provides. So, why didn't I just do what I knew I needed to do? What was this bind? One thing I knew for sure was that I needed to get back into my daily spiritual practice. Reading and talking the talk wasn't enough. I needed to practice what I preach. Do my spiritual work. I love Rev. Michael Beckwith's phrase, "It takes bliss-cipline!"

He then goes on to ask why we choose anxiety, fear, and negativity over joy. But what was this walk anyway? I started contemplating this. I decided to give it structure.

My daily spiritual diet begins with an affirmation. I shake them up for specific needs, but my current one is:

Today I have peace within. I trust I'm exactly where I'm meant to be. I remember the infinite possibilities available to me. I share my true gifts of compassion. I move forward today knowing this is my truth.

My day ends with a contemplative reminder around gratitude and forgiveness for my encounters that day or things I may need reminding.

I try to be the best parent I can be and where I fail, I give myself a break. I try hard to listen to my children. (This is so important!) I seek meaningful, authentic connections in my relationships with others. I seek first to understand. I practice graciousness. I try to do yoga and meditate daily. I want to exercise, for my heart's sake, more often, (this is a constant—am I alone in this?) I eat mostly healthfully and seek moderation in all other things I put into my body—whether this is organic or electronic or and anything in between. I observe. I seek stillness. I love to watch nature. I try to hang out in nature (hike, bike, kayak, ski, snowshoe—this last one is a current goal) at least once a week. I take my shopping cart back. I recycle. I say hello to people on the street. I play with my children (mostly projects—I'm not the hands-on, playing-with-trucks kind of mom). I adore my animals (I find them more entertaining than television). I make sure I have good sex regularly.

Some time ago I gave up all news (radio, television, Internet, and newspaper), and I still am pretty much in the loop, plugged in. It's astounding how much you learn without even trying. And it's plenty.

This is my spiritual diet; it doesn't mean that I don't struggle with other diet issues (diet is whatever I encounter with my body—persons, places, things) but I find that the more I keep up with my spiritual practice, the more the unhealthy behaviors or aspects of my daily diet fall away. All of these things help me stay clear on what I need, what I want, what I don't need, and what I don't want. And it deepens my relationships and my appreciation for life ... and my conscious connection with spirit.

Eck—Spectations!

I'm forgetting the part where I trip on this walk, when expectations come up. Expectations of myself. These are a big issue for me. I've known this about myself—that I have perhaps unreasonable expectations for myself that spill over into my expectations of others. I've had to work on this—this bloody wound—again and again. Simply put, these ideas fell under the guise of being perfect. Doing the right thing—the old perfectionism. Yet it wasn't what I preached. I was and am compassionate. "Give yourself a break." Again, I practice "seek first to understand." I knew my expectations of myself were unattainable, intellectually. Yet I found myself back at war with the "shoulds, woulds, and coulds." Things like, I should be a vegan, or I should be working on something with my daughter. (That's a regular. My secret plan for her fourth-grade year is to go on sabbatical to Italy only to avoid the science project I know is coming!) Or I should drive a Prius. I feel sick throwing out something that could be recycled. I had to feel more … do more … be more.

There is no winning in this line of thinking. It's circular. You end up where you began. The only way out is truth. Just be who you are (I'm seeing a slogan in my mind), and love yourself, *no matter what.*

It shows up in my relationships as disappointment. I experience disappointment when my expectations are off base. What can I do? I can't go through life having little or no expectations of others, though it would be nice and could eliminate disappointment. However, I can lessen this by truly seeing and accepting each person's journey as his or her own. This can be challenging. It involves letting go.

I say, "It can be lonely when you are doing deep work. You will lose people. There is a reason Jesus had disciples. As did Gandhi and many spiritual teachers. We need to surround ourselves with like minded people to support us. It is worth it, if you are on this path, which you clearly are because you are here. And there are many, many others joining you. People want to live a more spiritual life. Seek out others on the same path." I have incredibly talented, inspirational, intelligent and loving friends. That's who is on this path.

And my favorite unrepentant statement that I've said to others and myself many times: "It'll be okay."

It is scary. And it can feel like uninhabited terrain if you don't find community. It's one thing to live in books. It's another thing to deal with people; to have expectations of others. I've had to learn to modify, to open my eyes wider, clean out my ears, and pay attention. This hasn't always gone so well.

This is an aspect of my most common universal lesson—the one where I get kicked in the rear. When I have expectations and they aren't met, I am deeply hurt. Though the wound is old and familiar, it is my expectations that I can eventually see as the culprit. I didn't seek first to understand. I am too disappointed and wrapped up in my emotions. Then, I need to work on forgiveness for myself and the others in the situation. Again, the clarity is worth the journey.

This transparency naturally occurs if you practice stillness, observation, and meditation. Slowing down helps things come through. When we are running around keeping busy, we are just avoiding the things we don't want to come through. Pain—I don't want that. Avoidance—I want to be fully present. And again, accept people (and myself!) for wherever we are on our journey. This is the only true way to avoid the disappointment. Though it's not easy, I highly recommend it.

There it is. Just do it. Live an authentic life.

My Cleansing Coquinas Walk

I know shame. Or rather, I became completely reacquainted with it when the casino adventure occurred. Fortunately, I had some tools for this toxic feeling. Tools that helped me shed this quickly. Though I knew a lot about affirmations and accessing my own true self, sometimes it takes a little extra. I recommend a Zen activity, one that requires your entire focus. When time allows, this is a healing thing. I learned this by an experience that put me to the test.

I was vacationing in Puerto Vallarta, Mexico (one of my favorite places), with my family and friends. We were wandering around town, tequila tasting; our friends had family in the business there, so it was truly special. Being from Napa, we were experienced with tasting. Being an ACoA, I was inexperienced with tequila. (And tequila tasting with 100 percent blue agave is akin to fabulous wine tasting.)

On this day, in this country, on this vacation, we were having fun. I had no idea how much fun. Hours after we stopped tasting, we went to dinner, and I was slammed by intoxication. I was coherent and able to walk, not even sick that night or the next day. But my personality changed, and I was mean to my son—and apparently completely unaware of it. (If I ever overdrank, I was a weeper, not aggressive or mean—this was unspeakable.)

The next day, my husband told me everything, and I was flooded with horrible, shameful feelings. I apologized to everyone, including our friends and especially my son (he played it off like a good son and preadolescent would). Our friends said it wasn't so bad, and I didn't need to feel so awful. Well, being the ACoA and therapist, the very idea that I had too much to drink was mortifying. I had to get out—fast. *Move.* In fact, this was one of my first conscious experiences with the intensity and hideousness of this toxic shame feeling. I wouldn't wish it on anyone, yet it is so common. Some live with this feeling all of the time. I was so wracked with shame, I disappeared, as fast as I could. I had to get away from everyone. I couldn't even look at my son. I went for a walk on the beach. It was the only thing I could do. I felt so hideous. Unsightly. And any interaction with nature heals my soul.

As I began walking, my mind was alive and well, reinforcing my shame. "You are a bad person. How could you? What will they think? Oh, my God, you made a fool of yourself." And so on and so on and so on. As I walked, I also took in my surroundings. Watching the water, the children, the families in the water, the hotels, the merchants.

Eventually, I began to see coquinas on the beach. Coquinas are tiny shells, usually found open but attached. They are sweet. Like butterflies. I've collected lots of them on Sanibel Island (shell capital of the world) but not anywhere else. I bent down and picked one up. In that moment, I felt my first sense of relief. My mind was remembering my safe place on Sanibel, my childhood vacation spot. I kept walking, but instead of observing my surroundings, I was staring at the grainy sand. And my mind was subtly quieting. Any flicker of a little butterfly in my peripheral, and I would bend down and collect my precious coquina. As I began to focus my mind on the search, unconsciously, my negative and shameful thoughts became fewer and fewer. As these awful thoughts lessened, my disgraceful, tense feelings in my body were replaced with a relaxed emotion. Eventually, I was captivated by my search for my coquinas. My search became a hunt, until my pockets were full and coincidentally, my thoughts were positive and full of forgiveness.

This was a great lesson for me, and I use it in my psychotherapy practice. I encourage my clients to focus on activities in the same way, to calm the mind. I believe the best activities come from those that nurture the creative aspect of the soul. Painting is a perfect example because your thoughts must quickly focus on the action, especially with oil paints. Also, art becomes an expression of your unconscious emotions. I love horseback riding; love the connection I feel when I'm around horses, the sensitivity and soulfulness of these splendid beasts. And you must be careful with them. Keep your focus.

For me, skiing offers this exact bliss, as I am forced to solely concentrate on the activity, my skis, and the snow, or else I could get seriously hurt. I feel great mentally, physically, and spiritually after a challenging day on the mountain. When any activity demands your attention and thoughtfulness, it's healing.

The Clearing of the Clutter of the Chatter of the Mind

What a world this could be if we would take some time and just feel. And then take the time to think. Observe. Ponder. Reflect. Take time to be with these feelings; notice our thoughts, the ones that come up while we are practicing stillness. Kind of like prayer. And meditation. These practices force you to find clarity (and peace). Thomas Keating writes beautifully and usefully about contemplative prayer in his book *Open Mind, Open Heart: The Contemplative Dimension of the Gospel*. If you pick up this book (and I wholly endorse this holy man's work), chapter nine speaks directly to the benefits of prayer or meditation for anxiety caused by trauma,

"One way to deal with intense restlessness, physical pain, or emotions, such as fear or anxiety, that arise at such times of unloading is to rest in the painful feeling for a minute or two and allow the pain itself to be your prayer word. In other words, one of the best ways of letting go of an emotion is simply to feel it. Painful emotions, even some physical pains, tend to disintegrate when fully accepted …"[12]

Of course, we could possibly put addiction counselors out of business, yet we'd be authentic to ourselves. We would know what's really going on inside instead of reacting before we have a clue. Why are we so afraid of knowing and feeling what's going on inside? Whether it's a nick or a cut or a stab, the pain is relative. What is a nick for one person feels like a stab to another. Pain is pain. And it hurts.

Cutting has been around since before the pyramids. It is well documented. People (mostly adolescents) cut themselves in order to physical-ize the emotional pain that is inside them. The pain that cannot be seen. And it provides a release and feels good—it releases endorphins. I wouldn't pathologize these clients, for in some ways, they got it right. They are screaming, *"I am in pain."* I recommend they hold an ice cube for as long as possible, or wear a thick rubber band on their wrists that they can snap back and cause pain. Both exercises hurt, and both induce the endorphin response without scarring.

I explain, "Someday, you will be a happy, healthy twenty-five-year-old, and these scars will only remind you of a terrible time in your life. A time that doesn't define you."

I say it, knowing they are in the depths of despair, hoping to provide some light, if only a little. Unbeknownst to each other, my brother and I had a brief and benign dance with cutting when we were barely teens. Secretly and separately. We shared this with each other years later, in college. It was remarkable—at the same time that I was in my upstairs bedroom, he in his, downstairs. We didn't know about this until nearly a decade later, after the fact. I remembered scratching myself under my wrists and explaining it away as kitten cuts. Nothing major, but it helps me understand the why. For me and my brother, it was a cry for help, for recognition that something wasn't right. It was something we could see that revealed and affirmed our emotional pain.

When working with children, it is crucial the therapist uses art. Children put their thoughts on paper, this is how they clear their minds. It is equally useful for adults. Again, to aid in releasing the thoughts and feelings that are deep in our unconscious—the ones that may be cluttering up our potential for good. These activities open us up for our highest good to come through, our divine flow.

Table the Television

I've had an interesting love affair with television. In the seventies, I was the typical child who came home and watched *Bewitched* and *I Dream of Jeannie*—the good ones, the ones that had magic. In the eighties, it was great sitcoms. In the nineties, I barely watched television, as I was a busy single working parent. When I moved to Napa, we had to have cable to get any station—this was new to me, so I ordered the very basic cable. When my future husband came around, he convinced me that in order to watch the Olympics, which I love, I needed to increase my cable channels. I fell for it. A couple of years later, I became one of the original TiVo subscribers. And my television world exploded wide open. I watched more television than ever.

For me, television is a great escape. And in Napa, at the end of the day, I needed something mindless. The problem is that television encompasses all things and has the potential to exacerbate anxiety. It also takes time away from other practices that are better for me. For example, there was a time when I didn't censor my TiVo very well. Initially, I watched a lot of forensic television, because my husband liked this, and it was something we would watch together. I watched all of the *Law and Order* shows, anything with criminal behavior. This is not good for someone with anxiety. I loved soap operas (feels like a confession!), but they take a lot of time. I'm politically inclined (multiple generation political activism in my family), so the twenty-four-hour news cycle had great potential in my world, as well as the coverage of disasters. Now, I'm mad about Bravo, Discovery, Animal Planet, and Food Network.

I have had to table the television (though not completely) as part of my need for balance and moderation and as a part of my spiritual diet. I've periodically gone over my TiVo recordings and revised. I'm sure I could research why I chose what to record, based on what was happening that day or week. I can experience the craving for a good adrenaline show—*24* was actually too much for me—or a political fix—*Face the Nation, Meet the Press.*

I simply try not to engage in things that stir me up. But then, along came an interesting and compelling election. In my new state, there was a mystifying senate race. Nevada ranks very low in the nation in areas of education, and high in unemployment, and foreclosures, yet there was a tight race between someone in a position of power, who could bring lots to the state, and someone who would not have any power in Washington. Regardless of political party affiliation, if the state had needs, the choice should be easy. Yet one candidate, the freshman, gave the other, a senior, a serious run for his money. I was floored. And a little freaked out (where did we move?) And that day, I relapsed and plugged myself right back in to the twenty-four-hour news cycle. Well, let me tell you, it did not feel good. My heart was pumping a little differently all day, and I felt negative.

I hope I learned my lesson. Table the television.

Meditation, Not Mediation

Occasionally, though much less so in this new practice, I will see a couple referred for mediation. And I want to say, "Okay! Let's stop and meditate!" That probably would not go over well, although I'm certain it would help.

When I describe the benefits of meditation, I have a broad definition that is inclusive of all types. What I share is that meditation doesn't have to be what you may think it is—agony! You don't have to be good at sitting still; you don't have to even sit still.

In my practice, personal and professional, meditation is a tool for figuring out what negative thoughts need recognition, so they can be released. Recognition is difficult to do when we have ourselves plugged into everything these days. How do we hear our thoughts? And surely we are avoiding them when we sit watching the television, with our computer on, and our phone ringing all of the time. And isn't that the point? Yet we also are avoiding the voice of our true self. The one that knows we are a good and worthy person. Because our true self cannot be heard above the melodic ring tones or the busyness of our lives. You will not hear this truth if you are always on the go. You have to set aside time for peace and stillness. All of the other stuff prevents us from being fully conscious, although those negative thoughts are still getting through.

I have described this to many people when explaining the benefits of meditation and why it works. Meditation helps you get clear on the thoughts that are negative, the ones that are clogging your capacity for greatness. It doesn't mean you have to sit in a yoga position for hours on end. It just means slow down. Take your time. Observe.

Breathe. And listen.

Ah, Affirmations

Affirmations are positive thoughts written down, or memorized that can change the way you feel in an instant. My definition. I often write them for clients in the form of a mantra. For example, "I'm a good person; I'm a good worker; I'm a good daughter; I'm a good mother; I'm a good wife." I ask my clients to repeat this over and over, taking a breath before the last sentence of the mantra, so there is no breath between the ending and the beginning when repeating. I'm not sure why, but this works. I learned this breath trick many years ago and it has helped many. I most recommend mantras when we are being talked "at" by someone who is depleting us by criticism and/or negativity. Judgment. The mantra, recited in the mind—not aloud—prevents the negativity from getting in.

I once dated a man who had Post-it notes affixed in his car on his rearview mirror and his dashboard—affirmations. At the time, I must have been fairly unconscious (that is, unaware of my own true self), because I thought maybe there was something wrong with him. I was a reluctant dater—though I wanted a relationship, if there was any sign of weakness or weirdness, I was outta there. His Post-its frightened me off, because I actually thought this was odd. And I was totally in favor of affirmations at the time, working with and endorsing them regularly. I, obviously, wasn't ready to integrate them into my life, where they would be effective.

First, I had to integrate the very basic affirmation: *I deserve.* It's all about deserving. People get hung up on this word, this concept, in the most complex and the simplest ways. When I speak this word in my practice, my clients are moved to tears. The subject is interesting and intriguing yet sadly damaging and stifling. Years were wasted for me, but I get it now, and I can share it well. I hope.

I highly recommend affirmations as a tool for reminding ourselves of our true nature. And it is a quick way to help us change our thinking. It is the crux of Cognitive therapy. Replacing unhelpful thoughts with new positive thoughts works; it just takes work. When you have a negative thought about yourself (or someone else), you can replace it with something positive, if you take the time. This is so easy, yet so difficult for us to believe or accomplish. There are many books that provide great specific affirmations, but the book I most recommend is Louise Hay's *You Can Heal Your Life.* In this book, Hay lays out the illness or symptom, how it relates to your emotional issue, and an affirmation for healing.

I create affirmations for my clients that are specific to the issue that is keeping them from their higher self. I have my own pool of private affirmations for when I come up against personal challenges, the ones that come from the deep dark waters. This practice was getting lost in the mix as I was struggling with my authentic-self issues.

When I dismissed this man with the Post-its, it was because I wasn't accepting my own divinity, my true self. I was attending and reading, but I hadn't truly integrated these ideas into my daily life. I know this, because it scared me to see someone doing the work. I remember the first time I walked into a metaphysical church and the song they sang had the line, "I am beautiful." And then I got weepy. And then, defensively, I thought, *This is corny.* And I could barely tolerate sitting through the service. And then came the hand-holding and the hugs. Oh boy, this was a struggle. But I persevered and learned to love myself (and the music).

I have shared this many times. Our defense—sarcasm, kidding—is all about avoiding our true self. Marianne Williamson has a powerful poem about this, very popular. A copy has been in my day planner since the day I found it in 1996.

I will include only a portion: "Our deepest fear is not that we are inadequate. Our deepest fear is that we are powerful beyond measure. It is our light, not our darkness that most frightens us. We ask ourselves, who am I to be brilliant, gorgeous, talented, fabulous? Actually, who are you not to be? You are a child of God. Your playing small does not serve the world ..."

Believe in and love your true self.

Don't Buck the Buck

Pearl S. Buck said, "Sorrow fully accepted brings its own gifts. For there is alchemy in sorrow. It can be transmuted into wisdom which, if it does not bring joy, can yet bring happiness." [13]

This is another exemplification of Pema Chodron's comments from her book *When Things Fall Apart*, as well as the wisdom of many other enlightened people. It's the old lesson story. There is a lesson in every situation, a revealing. A demonstration. An opportunity. I've learned that my lesson in the examination of my casino experience, my moves, and my relationships is about living an authentic life. No matter what my behaviors are, I need to accept and love myself for who I am. And if I believe in the divine in all of us, how difficult can this be? There is some work involved, but it's worth it. It's like buying a beautiful, expensive pair of shoes (if we feel we deserve this) and for a while, they may hurt—financially, emotionally, and with blisters. After wearing them for some time, they start to feel comfortable, and we feel sexy. We begin to feel good about ourselves, even if there is a little doubt seeping in. Eventually, we put them on without thought, and walk a good strong walk. It all comes together. These unkind behaviors drop away as you begin to love yourself. Put on those sexy shoes.

Thank goodness. Thank God.

I remember telling a client, "Our blocks are our stepping stones that lead to bliss—joy and happiness. In between is the stuff of fear and anxiety."

How difficult is it to stay on the stones? Why do we choose to walk in the stuff?

As I'm thinking about this, I'm envisioning all those cracks in the sidewalks, and the superstitions, and people who succumb to the practice of stepping over them. This is about fear and anxiety. These cracks hold their fears, and this practice helps them avoid anxious feelings. In my efforts to avoid anxious feelings, my stepping stones were in a circle, leading me back to the same place. And this culminated in my final move. As I started seeing this, I began receiving these gifts. My creative spirit resurfaced; I started seeing things with a clarity that felt cleaner than any I'd known before. My "caring what people think" bubble burst—again! I just plain felt better about myself—no matter what I was up to.

The gift of loving yourself and accepting yourself and the gift of awareness—this one has a special bow.

Ahhhh ... the Om

Om *or aum is a mystical or sacred* syllable *in the* Indian religions (Hinduism, Buddhism, Sikhism *and* Jainism). *Aum is commonly pronounced as a* long or overly long nasalized, close mid-back rounded vowel, *though there are other enunciations pronounced in received traditions. It is placed at the beginning of most* Hindu texts *as a sacred incantation to be intoned at the beginning and end of a reading of the* Vedas *or prior to any prayer or* mantra. *The* Māndukya Upanishad *is entirely devoted to the explanation of the syllable. The syllable consists of three phonemes, a, u and m, which symbolize the beginning, duration, and dissolution of the universe and the associated gods* Brahma, Vishnu, *and* Shiva, *respectively.*)[14]

The way I explain the importance of the om is like this: "All religions, in separate times and locales, just happen to come up with a word for God that encompassed this sound—this vibration, this ahhh sound. Alaha, God, Adonai, Krishna, Buddha, Yeshua, Allah, Yaweh, Rama, Ra,

Abwoon, Rapha, Inanna … coincidence? I think not. And this vibration is available to all of us, this channel to God. It is within us. It is working through us. It is us. And it heals."

It is used in meditation. We can conjure up images of a person in a yoga position, hands curled open at the knees, chanting, "Ommmm." Well, this is great but not necessary. Any prayer or meditation works. Or chants. Or Hail Mary's. Or a hike through nature. The point isn't about meditation or quiet; affirmations provide the same clarity when used in repetition. This is about knowing and accessing the divine within us. Any of these practices provide the opportunity to take pleasure in this place of joy, bliss, and other feel-good experiences. Again, these practices lead to clarity and beauty because they eliminate the roughage of our daily lives—the thoughts and input that prevent our true selves from coming through. This is a gift from God (or whatever/however you experience this) to feel inner peace and joy. It is a blessing available to all of us.

My work was to get back to what I knew. To access this. My confusion was about authenticity. My belief was that as long as I was engaging in shameful behaviors, I couldn't access God. My authentic self. How silly. It was an either/or situation. Authenticity is about being true to myself, regardless of my behaviors. Yet for me, these behaviors were messing with my beliefs.

Rumi, an incredible teacher and Sufi mystic said, "From the day you born there was a ladder set up for you to escape." [15]

A ladder for you to access God. I know this quote. I use it often with my people. Why was I forgetting this?

I remember being in a collaborative meeting with people I admired and respected in Napa, years ago. I felt honored to be included, as I was young and the least experienced. One of the leaders wanted to take a break so she could smoke a cigarette. I was stunned. Didn't she need to hide this from all of these powerful people? Wasn't this going to be judged? Well, she was a highly regarded authentic person. Another time, over twenty-five years ago, I remember seeing a woman on a nude beach. Though she was fairly overweight, she walked with confidence and beauty. I thought to myself, *I want to be like her—beautiful, sexy, and unconcerned about my body. Authentic.* And I did the work, or so I thought. For a time, it was working—until my double-whammy grief, because that was when my remission was over.

New Thought, Not New Age

Ralph Waldo Emerson said, "Every spirit builds itself a house; and beyond its house, a world; and beyond its world a heaven. Know then, that the world exists for you: build, therefore, your own world." [16]

This, to me, is the beginning and essence of New Thought.

When I explain it to others, I must qualify it by saying, "It's not New Age." Because the term New Age is fraught with prejudice, even though as a movement, it encompasses the very same ideas and the science (quantum physics) that's behind New Thought. In my mind and experience, New Age was a movement in the seventies, a good delineator for a book wholesaler. New Thought is much older. Its origins, in addition to Emerson, include Thoreau, and Emma Curtis Hopkins and eventually, this became organized and structured by a prolific and enlightened man, Ernest Holmes. And it is talked about by many other mystics.

At the basis of all religions, you will find the principals of New Thought. For me, in my practice, I work with all religions, as New Thought can be adjunctive. I explain my philosophy to my clients when needed (for example, if their child is highly anxious because he believes the devil is lurking under his bed). They generally respond, "I can get on board with that." Because these principals work. They are the common denominator of all spiritual practices. And I also believe these clients are accepting because they are open to a new idea. Either they are desperate for a solution and will try anything; or they are curious about learning something new; or they trust me enough to take a risk. In any circumstance, I haven't experienced any backfire.

So why the prejudice? The resistance? Why does the idea of or the word *God* make some people ill at ease and others commit unloving acts in the name of religion? Why are we so segregated in an arena with so much universality? Undoubtedly ego, which has nothing to do with Spirit. And I am certain all of the great spiritual mystics would be horrified by some of the things that have occurred in their name.

It's Intentions

Wayne Dyer, in his most recent book, *The Invisible Force,* defines intention as "a field of energy that flows invisibly beyond the reach of our normal, everyday habitual patterns. It's a force that we all have within us, and we have the power to draw it into our lives by being the energy we want to attract."[17]

Dyer also has a great book called *The Power of Intention.* I have recommended it and worked it in my psychotherapy practice many times. And in my life. On the appropriate occasion, with certain clients, I share my intention story—how, when I was in graduate school, my dean asked me to write a letter to myself, based on where I wanted to be a year from now. What I wrote at the time seemed like I was asking for the moon. I had no idea how this was going to happen, but I took a leap of faith (again, I'd been a metaphysician since birth, which my dean did not know).

I wrote: *I want to be living in a town that feels safe, probably a small country-type town, where I could connect with a spiritual community and be successful in my work.*

Successful in my work is *huge* for me. It's not about the money but the belief that I am good at what I do—helping others.

One year later, walking away from my mailbox, I recognized the writing on the envelope as my own. I opened it up, perplexed. And I was astonished as I read it. I had just spent the weekend helping my Napa Center for Spiritual Living sandbag the place in case of a flood; I had a thriving practice; and I felt very safe there as a single parent. Napa gives you the feeling that you don't have to lock your doors. It was amazing. And validating. *Intentions work.* (And Napa was completely off my radar screen when I wrote it.)

About fifteen years ago, I attended a workshop called "Dare to be Great," facilitated by Terri Cole-Whittaker, which was also the title of her book. She asked us to write down our greatest intention—where did we see ourselves in the future? What were we doing?

"Think big! Be specific!" she said. "We don't think grand enough!"

I wrote down: *I want to write a book that will help others, and I see myself talking with Oprah about it on her stage, in her studio.* This was a definite fantasy, though I thought (hoped) I'd be a writer by the time I was in my forties, after I launched my son off to college.

I saw myself as a writer (I wrote regularly), so this artistic path was easy for me. I could write for anybody else. Cover letters, dialogue, articles, plays. Honestly, my family said if I wanted to make a lot of money, I should have gone into advertising. Well, I have rarely watched live television, so I don't see commercials—as a TiVo subscriber, it's all about skipping the advertisements. I knew I was a writer, yet when it came to the intimacy of self-help, I was challenged, to say the least. And it was shocking. I honestly thought I would leave my Napa practice and write a fabulous book, based on my fabulous women. But I became stuck. (Michael Beckwith says we have intention deficit disorders—I love this!) It's much easier for me to write comedy and fiction. Boy, was this different.

Yet my intention *had* been set, and then the universe (and the power of shame) provided!

Not-So-Sneaky Synchronicity

I see synchronicity in all matters. Wikipedia defines synchronicity as *the* experience *of two or more* events *that are apparently* causally unrelated *or unlikely to occur together by chance, that are observed to occur together in a* meaningful *manner. The concept of synchronicity was first described by* Swiss psychologist Carl Gustav Jung *in the 1920s.*[18]

Synchronicity is striking around grief. I believe because of the law of attraction. As we are experiencing this profound transition in our lives, we are attracting similar situations. The universe is placing things in our path at the right time. When my brother died, there was a particular couple whom my parents knew, though not very well. This couple owned a condo in the building where my sister had owned a unit at Lake Tahoe. When my sister moved back to New York City, my parents bought my sister's condo and lived there while renovating their house. The other couple mostly lived in San Francisco and would come up to the lake on occasion. Turned out, my brother had worked for the wife years before. When he died, the couple reached out to my parents because of the condo neighbor connection—they hadn't realized at that time that the wife had actually known my brother, and when they did, their friendship grew deeper.

On the one-year anniversary of my brother's death, the husband's brother died in a tragic accident. This solidified their great and longstanding friendship with my parents, one that holds a permanent place in my parents' address book.

My brother and Scott each were working at a Whole Foods, though at different stores in different counties, when they died. This synchronicity was a great comfort to me, as Whole Foods was a community. And people from Whole Foods, who didn't know my brother but knew me through Scott, sent me many condolences when he died.

Synchronicity and the unconscious. Surprising stuff. I had a client who had a dream about my house. There was a circus in my backyard. The easy, psychodynamic answer is that she wanted to be with me, in my house. Plain and simple. Her details about my house were spot on. The astounding part was that I had a similar dream. That same week. A dream that a circus train (like Barnum and Bailey) had come through my fence, and there were people charging admission at the door of my broken fence to see the circus.

Now, we could analyze this dream to kingdom come, and it'd be fund, yet my only analysis is about the circus. We had just moved into our new house, and the day we moved in was extremely windy, and one of our fences blew down. The following day, we received eighteen inches of snow and record cold temperatures. Was the weather feeling like a circus? And was my client plugged into this? Or was it my crazy idea to move into a house I fell in love with on the brink of the worst real estate market ever. Was my life beginning to feel like a circus? And don't forget the compulsion to move, following the sorrow on my last street. I do believe my client and I were accessing each other in the unconscious realm, constellating our mutual grief experiences.

As I was working on this book, a friend sent me a link to one of her dear friend's *New York Times* book reviews, *Chasing Daylight* by Eugene O'Kelly. It's about the author's "death plan," which he created after finding out he had untreatable brain cancer and limited time. His subtitle: *Seize the power of every moment.* Although I am simplifying this, it goes to the synchronicity aspect. I'm writing a book about grief and authenticity, where I've written a chapter that includes a paragraph on how nice it would be to have a death plan, and here a book on the subject arrives. And the book is remarkable, as is synchronicity, if we open ourselves to it. My friend had no idea what my book was about at the time she sent the link.

I explain synchronicity to my clients, very simply, in the following way:

"Let's say I recommend a book title to you, and after you leave my office, you go to the grocery store. The woman in line at the cashier in front of you has a book in her purse, and you can see the title—it's the book I told you to buy. Notice this. The universe is telling you to read this book."

Once you learn to open your awareness in this way, great things happen. You start seeing your path as it is inviting you, pointing you in the right direction.

So, It's Spirituality

For me, spirituality is broad and encompasses our relationship with that which connects us to something greater. This can be a secular religious practice or a walk in the woods. Yoga. Gardening. Introspection and action. Time spent in peace. Whenever there is no more clutter and the inner voice, the spirit of your true self can come through. The divine, who knows you are a good and beautiful person. Again, it is difficult to hear this voice when you are a busy person on the move. It requires solitude. For me, my spiritual life, family, and professional life share equal parts. That's just how it is. And that's how I like it. I feel guilty sometimes that my family doesn't have the typical structured life (dinner at six, all together) because of my work. I know if I am fulfilled, though, that those around me will be happier, because I am.

I believe that healing from your childhood issues (and we all have them) or trauma takes spiritual work, beyond the psychological piece. Though I can't live like a monk, I can create a peaceful environment and incorporate these practices that nurture my divine.

You know how when you eat something healthy—say, a bowl of steel-cut oatmeal with fresh fruit—you think, *I'm healthy. My body feels good.*

Or when you have a good, hard workout, you think, *I'm in great shape. My body feels great and works well.*

Or you come up with a brilliant idea, you think, *Damn, I'm smart.*

In reality, eating healthy, exercising, and working your brain will *eventually* produce positive results, yet the instant reality is also the case. You feel good—regardless of whether or not the actual long-term results have been integrated—because this is effective.

That's how spiritual practice works. It feeds itself, in all aspects of the self. Prayer, meditation—any practice that brings conscious awareness (like therapy). It has instant results. Most people feel better upon leaving their therapist's office than when they arrived. This is because of the safe environment. This is true for meditation and spirituality. The bliss, the love, comes through. It's the quintessential piece, after all. It just is. It is not a result or a variable; it is ever present. And accessible to all.

I tend to investigate joy when I'm trying to help someone who is spiritually challenged. Joy is, to me, where the creative aspect of spirit is expressed. For some, it's easy. For others, it's screaming to come out, but it's tightly locked away. I remember driving through parts of Oakland, California, and seeing the incredibly creative graffiti around me. I thought about how these spirits were expressing themselves, most likely despite adverse conditions in their lives. It's an important aspect of our spirits. It feels good and is healing when we demonstrate our creativity. I express my creativity in writing. And I love to sing and dance. When I'm at a rock concert, I hardly ever sit down. I won't miss an opportunity to see my legends—Elton John, Carlos Santana—because again, *it feels so good!*

With many clients, I discuss spirituality and religion at some point. Some therapists would say this is a no-no. Many psychotherapy practices avoid God. Yet it's an important part of our vitals. I wonder, where is God in your address book? Is it in the obvious G section, or J for Jesus? Or is it under S for Spirit? A for agnostic, atheist, or Allah? N for nature? Or is it erased … or was it ever there?

My passion for the power of metaphysics is inevitably thrown into the mix of dialogues about God. Again, I wholeheartedly believe in these principles. It is deeply a part of my life and comes through in my work, though perhaps more through the back door than the front.

Just a Gull Named Jonathan

Whenever I see seagulls on the beach or in the garbage of a city, I call out, "Jonathan!" This embarrasses whoever is with me to no end, but I love it. It's a spiritual reminder. In Richard Bach's book, *Jonathan Livingston Seagull*, Jonathan is a student (and a bird) on a path of life lessons. And he has some misconceptions about himself. Some inauthentic beliefs. There are many concepts in this book (which is a favorite of mine) that resonate with the work I found myself attending to: cliques, teachers, flight (PTSD), forgiveness, among others. When I recommend spiritual practice to clients I tell them:

"This isn't necessarily about prayer or meditation only. It's also about reminders. Icons, books, rocks, (I collect heart rocks), affirmations on Post-its, anything that reminds you of your connection with Spirit—that brings it conscious. In my house, I have something in every room and sometimes many items that bring me instantly to my spiritual place, just by seeing them. It's so helpful. And it's personal to me—no one else. Anyone could see what I see and not make the connection. But I do. And that's what matters. Make it personal to you."

In my house, you may see an altar. You may see a sculpture. A rock. A cross. A painting. A magnet. Buddha. Certain books in special places. A drawing by my son or daughter. A photograph. These are visual reminders for me, affirmations for myself, of where I come from. Where I am going. Where my life is today. Where my highest good is operating. And it keeps me focused, in this age of distractedness. These are good things.

These are beautiful reminders of my relationship with my source as well as reminders of how I am meant to live my highest good.

Oh, For the Love of God

L ove. So easy yet so difficult for some. Wikipedia defines love as *an* emotion *of strong* affection *and personal* attachment. *In philosophical context, love is a* virtue *representing all of human* kindness, compassion, *and affection. Love is central to many* religions, *as in the Christian phrase,* "God is love" *or* Agape *in the* canonical gospels. *Love may also be described as actions toward others (or oneself) based on compassion. Or as actions toward others based on affection.* [19]

Compassion. Full circle. Love and understanding. My work here.

My *Webster's* defines love as a verb: *to hold dear, cherish; to feel a lover's passion, devotion, or tenderness; to fondle amorously; to copulate with; to like or desire actively; to take pleasure in; to thrive in; to feel affection or experience desire* (Sounds like permission for all things sexual; I'm all for this!)

Interesting. To me, love is an expression of all things God, however that looks. Again, my picture: beauty, peace, intelligence, light, life, love, wisdom. It's in all things, this thing called love. You can find it even in the darkest of circumstances, because you can't have dark without light. It's impossible.

And trust. How does this come into play? Do you need trust in order to love? I think so. Trust in yourself, your true divine self. This seems complex yet once you get it, it's like riding a bicycle. Or a horse. Or putting on makeup or fabulous shoes.

When you lose important and intimate people when you are young, you become intensely and often unconsciously guarded. I share with my clients that I don't think I can ever fully trust another human. That's just a fact of my life. Maybe it's existential, but I think it's possibly true for all humans. I do wholeheartedly trust in God. In my loving spirit. It's unfailing. And that has come naturally to me. And although I love and trust my husband, I cannot feel wholeheartedly secure with him. After all, one of us will leave the other at some point. There are no guarantees from the time we are born. There's an end game in our human experience, but not in our spiritual. And certainly not with love. It has no beginning or ending. It just is—if we let it be. These beliefs have helped me survive the most difficult pain in my life. And for me, it is a scientific fact--spirit doesn't begin with birth or end with death.

What I learned from my dance with grief (which culminated in the casino) was to embrace what I already knew to be true. There is one life. God. Love. And that life is my life now. I got off track somewhere along the way through my many grief experiences. My track (path) was about love. Loving myself. Acting with love and kindness toward myself and, of course, others. It's easy for me to love my clients. In my grief, having PTSD symptoms, in the midst of how this was affecting my life, I lost sight of myself. My true self.

We often forget to love ourselves first. We get the reminder on the airplane: "Please put the oxygen mask on yourself first, so you can take care of your child." Yet we don't do this in our everyday lives.

Today, I am putting my mask on first again. And hopefully, I'm helping others to do the same. I love this statement made by Christiane Northrup, MD:

"Loving everything about yourself—even the unacceptable—is an act of personal power. It is the beginning of healing."

I had an inaccurate belief system about authenticity. I thought being authentic meant doing the right thing, and anything that made me feel like I wasn't doing this made me believe I was being inauthentic.

Living an authentic life is loving and being your authentic self.

Exit Stage Left, Epilogue

During the writing of this book, there were many minutes or hours, in the middle of the night or the wee hours of the morning, where I would think about my process. I would go over my timeline of my life in terms of my grief and trauma, my relationships, and my many moves. It was sad to think that I compounded a difficult situation by robbing myself of support. That it was easier for me to start all over again than to allow my past and others in. Yet, I chose to become a psychotherapist because of my propensity for intimacy and authenticity. For truth.

I also found myself worrying about people in my life and how they would receive this—my truth. I thought about James Frey and how he suffered in what I believe was a miscarriage of something. We all have our own truths. This is mine. My perceptions of my own life. In order to tell my story authentically, I tried to tell it as I remembered it, though I found myself getting hung up on factual dates and similar points. This story is my story.

My hope, in writing this, is to help others understand the depth of our work—and that *it is* work. But it is worth it. To know your true self (divine), to accept and forgive your human self—a gift worth fighting for. I will forever be on this path, doing this work, as it doesn't take much to knock us off.

My wish is that when you feel yourself complaining or having a negative feeling toward a stranger (or even someone you know) that you will think about the possibility that the person may be grieving. After all, in some way, we all are.

P.S. The Big Q

Do my husband and I still gamble? Yes, though much less so, and most likely when someone is visiting. And I don't ruminate about it anymore. Today, I can have fun in a casino, guilt-free, because I did the work, even though I am still irrational and seek jackpots when I gamble.

My examination of this, my confession, is that the casino country club adventure, and subsequent shame I experienced, was a blessing. It revealed the leftover grief piece churning inside. And my false belief that I was somehow being inauthentic because I was engaging in something I thought was wrong and unhealthy. I can just be my good and grateful self. I thank God I didn't enter this arena as a young, unconscious person. What a nightmare that could have been. Thank goodness for awareness.

P.P.S. Another Ancient Math Dude

I will leave one more verse from another ancient mathematician and astronomer (I highly recommend the entire version), Omar Khayyam (eleventh century), from *The Rubáiyát:*

If my coming here were my will, I would not have come.
Also, if my departure were my will, how should I go?
Nothing could be better in this ruined lodging,
Than not to have come, not to be, not to go.[20]

My Most Recommended Books/Authors

A New Earth, Eckhart Tolle

Adult Children of Alcoholics, Janet G. Woititz

Ageless Body, Timeless Mind, Deepak Chopra

The Anatomy of the Spirit, Carolyn Myss

The Artist's Way, Julia Cameron

Care of the Soul, Thomas Moore

Dare to Be Great, Terri Cole-Whitaker

The Four Agreements, Don Miguel Ruiz

Healing the Shame That Binds You, John Bradshaw

Owning Your Own Shadow, Robert A. Johnson

Men Are from Mars, Women Are from Venus, John Gray

Peace Is Every Step, Thich Nhat Hahn

The Power of Intention, Wayne Dyer

The Road Less Traveled, M. Scott Peck

Simple Abundance, Sarah Ban Breathnach

The Three-Minute Meditator, David Harp and Nina Smiley

What the Bleep Do We Know!?, William Arntz, Betsy Chasse, and Mark Vicent

You Can Heal Your Life, Louise Hay

Notes

1. Galilei Galileo. In Wikiquote, from http://en.wikiquote.org/wiki/Galileo_Galilei. As translated in The Philosophy of the Sixteenth and Seventeenth Centuries (1966) by Richard Henry Popkin. Website accessed August 01, 2012.

2. American Psychiatric Glossary (7th ed.), Edgerton, Jane E. (Ed); Campbell III, Robert J. (Ed), Washington, DC, US: American Psychiatric Press, Inc. (1994).

3. Webster's New Collegiate Dictionary, G. & C. Merriam Co., (1974)

4. Harold and Maude. In Wikipedia, from http://en.wikipedia.org/wiki/Harold_and_Maude. Website accessed August 01, 2012.

5. Pema Chödrön, When Things Fall Apart: Heart Advice for Difficult Times. Shambhala Publications, Inc. (1997).

6. Elisabeth Kübler-Ross, On Death and Dying (New York: Macmillan, 1969).

7. American Psychiatric Association. DSM–IV; Diagnostic and Statistical Manual of Mental Disorders (4th ed., text rev.). Washington, DC: Author (1994).

8. Epinephrine. In Wikipedia, from http://en.wikipedia.org/wiki/Epinephrine. Website accessed August 01, 2012.

9. J. G. Woititz. Adult Children of Alcoholics. Health Communications, Inc. (1990).

10. Psychobabble. In Wikipedia. from http://en.wikipedia.org/wiki/Psychobabble. Website accessed August 01, 2012.

11. Codependence, In Psychology Wiki, from http://psychology.wikia.com/wiki/Codependency. Website accessed August 01, 2012.

12. Thomas Keating. Open Mind, Open Heart: The Contemplative Dimension of the Gospel. St. Benedict's Monastery (1986 and 1982).

13. Pearl S. Buck. In Goodreads, from http://www.goodreads.com/quotes/30872-sorrow-fully-accepted-brings-its-own-gifts-for-there-is, Website accessed August 01, 2012.

14. Om, In Wikipedia, from http://en.wikipedia.org/wiki/Om. Website accessed August 01, 2012.

15. Rumi. In Baumwoll Archives, from http://baumwollarchives.com/quotations-of-the-day. Website accessed August 01, 2012.

16. Ralph Waldo Emerson. In Goodreads, from http://www.goodreads.com/quotes/26773-every-spirit-builds-itself-a-house-and-beyond-its-house. Website accessed August 01, 2012.

17. Dr. Wayne W. Dyer. The invisible Force: 365 Ways to Apply the Power of Intention to Your Life. (Hay House, Inc. September 1, 2007).

18. Synchronicity. In Wikipedia, from http://en.wikipedia.org/wiki/Synchronicity. Website accessed August 01, 2012.

19. Love. In Wikipedia, from http://en.wikipedia.org/wiki/Love. Website accessed August 01, 2012.

20. Omar Khayyam. From http://daylightsmark.blogspot.com/2011/02/selectionsfrom-rubaiyat-omar-khayyam.html. Website accessed August 01, 2012.

Introducing...

M Y S E L F H E L P
TOO

A new book series for those who have experienced the loss of a loved one. When I gave the first draft of my book MYSELF HELP to a focus group, the number one comment I received was that it was a helpful support group in a book. I liked this idea, especially understanding, personally, how lonely the process of mourning can be. It is a comfort knowing there are others who have shared grief experiences. This is the beauty of support groups, the collective knowledge. You are not alone.

Your story can be anonymous or not, that is up to you. If you would like, you can write your own brief bio to be included. If your story is edited, we will work on this with you.

Your submissions should include MYSELF HELP, too in the subject line and be sent to DanaAnderson.MFT@gmail.com. Please include your contact information. We graciously appreciate your heartfelt and inspirational stories.

Many Blessings,
Dana Anderson

CPSIA information can be obtained at www.ICGtesting.com
Printed in the USA
BVOW082043120213

313088BV00002B/3/P

9 781452 559582